More Praise for *Happiness from the Inside Out*

"*Happiness from the Inside Out* reads like a conversation with a cherished friend — a friend who gets you, levels with you, and supports you, while sharing of himself in generous, brave, and authentic ways. Wrap Rob Mack's heartfelt wisdom around you, and you'll have every insight you need to create true and lasting happiness."

> — Lisa McCourt, bestselling author of
> the Chicken Soup for Little Souls series

"Rob Mack has inspired and motivated me, helping me achieve goals I thought were out of reach. This book will be an asset to you in your daily life and help your growth exponentially!"

> — Chris Williams, actor

"There are plenty of life coaches out there, but Robert Mack is a jewel among coaches! His book is profound, powerful, and easy to understand. Kudos, Rob! Thank you for giving us this gem."

> — Veronica Conway, author of *The Black Paper*
> and creator of The Black Mastery Program

"Seeking happiness can seem like a trivial pursuit, especially in today's crisis-laden world. But Robert Mack's message, that fulfillment comes from within and can be easily cultivated, is right on time. Mack insists that finding happiness is worth the effort, and *Happiness From the Inside Out* is worth the read."

> — Caroline Clarke, editor-at-large,
> *Black Enterprise* magazine

"If you want to be happy for the rest of your life, Robert Mack will show you the way. Mack shows us that the pursuit of happiness, love, and success starts and ends with two very important letters: M-E. Mack delivers a book that teaches us that we have been looking for the secrets to success, love, and happiness in all the wrong places, and helps us see that the answers to lasting happiness are right inside ourselves."

— Christine Arylo, inspirational catalyst and author of *Choosing ME before WE: Every Woman's Guide to Live and Love*

Happiness from the Inside Out

Happiness from the Inside Out

The Art and Science of Fulfillment

ROBERT MACK

Foreword by Vanessa Williams

New World Library
Novato, California

New World Library
14 Pamaron Way
Novato, California 94949

Text design by Tona Pearce Myers

Library of Congress Cataloging-in-Publication Data
Mack, Robert.
Happiness from the inside out : the art and science of fulfillment /
Robert Mack ; foreword by Vanessa Williams.
    p.   cm.
Includes bibliographical references and index.
ISBN 978-1-57731-658-9 (pbk. : alk. paper)
 1. Happiness. 2. Self-actualization (Psychology) I. Title.
BF575.H27.M33 2009
150.19'88—dc22   2009003180

First printing, April 2009
ISBN 978-1-57731-658-9
Printed in Canada on 100% postconsumer-waste recycled paper

New World Library is a proud member of the Green Press Initiative.

10   9   8   7   6   5   4   3   2

Contents

Foreword

first met Rob Mack on the set of the short-lived series *South Beach*, which aired on what became the CW. In the pilot, Rob played a "boy toy" for my character. In one scene, his character had to rough up my character in a nightclub. He completed his mission during that one day of shooting, and I didn't see him again for five months. Then one afternoon, I was having lunch with my daughter on Lincoln Road in Miami, when Rob stopped by our table and reminded me of our encounter on-screen. I recognized him immediately. How could I forget that radiant smile?

Over the next few months while I was shooting in

Florida, Rob and I got together often for long discussions about life, love, and personal choice. I was thoroughly convinced that this bright, eager mind had a message to spread. Rob is an honest, open man of color, brought up in a world of differences, looking to make sense of it all. And, we hope, to give solutions to others with hearts and ears open to solve their problems.

At the time, Rob was consumed with a quest to understand happiness. We often spoke of how everyone strives for happiness but all too often have no idea what real happiness looks like or feels like, so to speak. In fact, I told Rob a few stories about my own discoveries of what did and didn't bring happiness.

When I told Rob these stories, we agreed that many people have had similar experiences. You may have had them yourself, experiences that were outrun by ballooning expectations of how an event or person or job would forever change you and make you eternally happy. Yet later you realize that you're no better off than before, the dog still needs to be walked, and the laundry still needs to be done. So then you set a new goal, but that one doesn't make you permanently happy either; that happiness, too, is short-lived.

You may assume, like many of us assume, that happiness is success — professional success, romantic success, financial success, physical success, or even spiritual success. Or you may think that success — in any or all of those forms — will bring happiness. But does success really cause happiness? Over the course of my life, I've had many thoughts about this: "Maybe," I've often pondered, "success isn't happiness. Maybe getting what you want isn't happiness either. Maybe happiness is something more, or something else."

When I talked with Rob about these thoughts, I realized that he had asked many of the same questions, and he had gone on to ask even more. In fact, Rob's approach to life, like his coaching practice, is always in the form of a question. If happiness is ultimately what we all strive for, then why don't we each spend more time learning about what happiness really is, how to get it, and where to find it? Why do we spend more time thinking about, talking about, and making decisions about where to eat, what car to drive, what career to pursue, where to live, what clothes to wear, who to date and marry, and, what's worse, what other people are eating, driving, pursuing, wearing, and doing? Why do we spend more time discussing what's going wrong in our lives than we do discussing what's going right in our lives?

Rob was so intrigued by these questions that he obtained a master's degree in positive psychology in an effort to quench his thirst for answers to these age-old questions. His coaching practice, too, is aimed squarely at helping others answer these questions, or questions like them, for themselves. This book allows Rob to help you by guiding you to find your own answers, just as he found his own answers. Welcome Rob's writing into your mind and heart, sit with this book and allow him to share his insights about how you might create a happier, healthier, and wealthier life from the inside out.

As you read this inspiring book, allow yourself to be shown the tools that can help you achieve awareness and confidence in the outside world. Realize that happiness is ultimately your own responsibility, but let an expert — Rob Mack — show you a few shortcuts. I know that if you listen closely to what he has to say and apply his principles to your life every day, you will achieve unprecedented success and unfathomable happiness in your life. It's a lot easier than you think. But you have to keep an open mind and an open heart. You have to practice patience and perseverance.

Rob's insights and practical advice will not disappoint you. Now if only they could bottle that radiant smile of his!

— Vanessa Williams, actress and singer

Introduction

We all live with the objective of being happy; our lives are all different and yet the same.

— ANNE FRANK

What would make you live happily ever after?

When I ask people this question, most of them answer it by listing things they want. They basically tell me that for them, happiness will come when they get these things. This line of thinking seems logical enough, but is it true? If it is true, the majority of people living in the United States, Canada, Europe, and large parts of Asia should be euphoric.

As Gregg Easterbrook describes in his book *The Progress Paradox*, the past fifty years have been a period of unprecedented economic and material growth. Most objective measures, even taking into account current economic downturns, point to overwhelming and unparalleled improvements in the quality of our lives. Look around. Average citizens enjoy the kinds of luxuries that our grandparents never imagined, much less had. Crime is, and has been, on the decline. Technology is better than ever, and we are seeing the result of that technological progress in both the quality and the longevity of our lives. We are, for the most part, living healthier and longer than ever before. The point here is clear: more folks are getting what they want, at least in a material sense, than at any previous time in history.

And yet, way too many people are unhappy. In fact, we've never before known so many unhappy people. Many indicators point to the same conclusion: people are less happy than they should be or could be or have been in the past. Unipolar depression is ten times more common than ever, teenage suicides are at an all-time high, and the average age at which people first experience depression has slipped from twenty-nine years of age to fourteen and a half years of age.

Even for average U.S., European, and Japanese citizens — people who are not experiencing severe mental dysfunction such as clinical-grade depression — happiness self-ratings have stood still for the past fifty years. Highlighting this remarkable finding, folks in the know are actually referring to the current era as "the revolution of satisfied expectations" at the same time that they are calling it "the age of melancholy." That is an interesting, unfortunate, and dangerous paradox.

If things — from a broad perspective — are better than ever and so good on the outside, why do so many of us feel so bad on the inside? Further, why are some of the richest, most famous, most successful people spinning into downward spirals of depression and self-destruction only to lose everything they've worked so hard, long, and passionately to achieve?

Why are so many people feeling worse as their lives have gotten better? More importantly, what can be done about it?

Myths of Happiness

Most people are unhappy, I believe, because they live their lives according to two big myths. The first myth is that life is about reaching a destination. "If we can only make it to the island," we think, "then life will be perfect." This myth mistakenly tells us that "success" is, by and large, the point of life. The second myth works hand in hand with the first one. It suggests that success — that is, getting what you want — will lead to happiness.

These myths are terribly misleading. They are so powerful and commonly accepted that they cause us to ignore what we know to be true, deep down: that happiness comes from the inside. Instead they lead us to focus on the outside, on destinations and success, which is a sure recipe for unhappiness.

In the movie *Fight Club*, Brad Pitt's character, Tyler Durden, explains what these myths have done to us:

Man, I see in fight club the strongest and smartest men who've ever lived. I see all this potential, and I see it squandered. God damn it, an entire generation pumping gas, waiting tables; slaves with white collars. Advertising has us chasing cars and clothes, working jobs we hate so we can buy shit we don't need. We're the middle children of history, man. No purpose or place. We have no Great War. No Great Depression. Our Great War's a spiritual war . . . our Great Depression is our lives. We've all been raised on television to believe that one day we'd all be millionaires, and movie gods, and rock stars. But we won't. And we're slowly learning that fact. And we're very, very pissed off.

Actually, Tyler Durden has it only half right. Even the people who *are* millionaires, movie gods, and rock stars are pissed off. It seems like the glass is half empty for almost everybody.

Happiness requires that we expose these two myths for what they are and learn the truth. That's what this book is about. In the chapters to follow, I will discuss what happiness really is, where to look for it, and how to get it. But more than that, I will explain why much of what you think about happiness is wrong and counterproductive. Reading this book, then, may prove to be one of the most disillusioning — and therefore rewarding — experiences of your life.

Happiness Is a Science

It used to be that good advice on how to go about seeking happiness came mostly from poets, philosophers, and clergymen. But within the past ten years, science has taken up happiness as its subject. In the fields of psychology and cognitive science, researchers have been turning away from their former focus on treating mental illness and instead investigating what it takes for psychologically "normal" people to feel satisfied, fulfilled, and genuinely happy. What they are finding has proven so useful that a whole new field, called positive psychology, has popped up, along with undergraduate courses and graduate programs. The most popular class at Harvard, for example, is a class in positive psychology taught by Tal Ben-Shahar. There are graduate programs in positive psychology at the University of Pennsylvania, Claremont Graduate University, Lewis University in Illinois, and other campuses.

One of the most important contributions of the new science of happiness has been to debunk all sorts of common notions about what should make us live happily ever after. You may think, for example, that financial success will guarantee you happiness — that hitting the lottery, living a life of luxury and leisure, driving an expensive car, or wearing brand-name clothes and jewelry will do the trick. Although money does help many people live happier lives, statistically speaking, the truth is that you need more than just financial success to be truly and lastingly happy. Happiness depends on a lot of other moving parts, some of which are controllable and some of which aren't controllable, and all of which are very personal and case specific.

You may believe that relationship success will guarantee you happiness. You may be convinced that getting married and having kids will bring you satisfaction and contentment. Or, perhaps you thought that becoming famous or getting people to like you or respect you would make you feel better about yourself and your life. Again, you'd be wrong.

You might think that professional success or winning lots of awards will bring you fulfillment and lasting happiness. You may believe that you'd be happier if you were blessed with a model's body and movie-star good looks. Or you may think that happiness will be found by experiencing as much pleasure as possible through sex, drugs, alcohol, partying, extreme sports, and so on. No, these things probably won't, by themselves, make you happy either.

These are all outside-in approaches to happiness. The science of happiness says that, by and large, they don't work.

Right Game, Wrong Rules

Most of us think that if we play it by the book and do what well-meaning and intelligent people have told us, we'll live happily ever after. We never consider that "the book" might be wrong. Life is not like preschool. It is not a meritocracy, and we don't get rewarded in real life just because we try hard. Happiness is more elegant than that; it takes more finesse. If happiness is a science, it is also an art.

Since most of us never question the assumptions by which we live our lives or the rules with which we conduct ourselves, we just keep trying harder. Our best never seems to be good enough. And boy is that frustrating! There's nothing more frustrating than believing your best just wasn't or isn't good enough. I would know. I lived the better part of my life doing just that: being frustrated and playing by the wrong rules.

The truth of the matter is that you have probably been working too hard for too long at the wrong things. And your life is living proof that this is true.

In nature, there are no rewards and punishments. There is only what you do and what you don't do. There are only consequences. If you're unhappy, in pain, or feeling frustration, these negative emotions are signs that something is wrong. You are meant to succeed. Failure, sickness, poverty, loneliness, and so on *should* feel bad. Something is wrong. But it's not the circumstances of your life; what's wrong is the consciousness that created those circumstances.

The purpose of this book is to show you how to intelligently and deliberately create an authentically happy — and, thus, successful — life. You create that kind of life by getting happy first, starting from the inside.

This book is the culmination of twelve years of research and practice, both professional and personal. If you successfully apply the principles outlined in this book, you will find yourself increasingly happier. What's more, you will find that happiness, more than anything else, is what leads to success. This has been shown to be true by more than a decade of research. Successful people are, by and large, happy first.

The principles in this book have been empirically proven and scientifically validated. They have worked for people from all walks of life. Their effectiveness rests not on the merits of the principles themselves but instead on how effectively and consistently you apply them to your life on a moment-by-moment basis. If you follow what's outlined here, I promise you will find a level of happiness and success unknown by the vast majority of men and women in the world.

Happiness can be learned. That said, I won't necessarily teach you anything all that new in this book. You've probably heard everything I have to say somewhere before. Even if you haven't heard it before, it may feel as if you have because it will resonate with the very core of your being and the very essence of who you really are. I will not be breaking new ground. Instead, I will be reminding you of what you knew when you were born into this body, of what you already know about being happy but may have forgotten, of who you already are but may not be remembering or appreciating — a happy, healthy, wealthy individual with the answers to all your individual questions inside. I will help you figure out where you took that wrong turn and how to get back on track, in flow, and on course. More than anything, then, I will be leading you back to the guidance system that exists within you, your own very unique happiness positioning system. I will be leading you back to yourself.

The Principles

Through a combination of acts of will, you can change your happiness level substantially. But there isn't just one secret or key to happiness. As with caring for the physical body, you need a variety of vitamins and nutrients, not just one or two. This book is built around eight principles for creating a happier life. Each one builds on the one before it, and they all rest on a simple premise: that happiness must be your ultimate goal.

1. *The principle of smart energy investment:* Invest your time and energy in ways that bring the highest happiness return.
2. *The principle of nonattachment:* Detach your happiness from specific results, circumstances, or outcomes.
3. *The principle of positive focus:* Give your conscious attention to the better-feeling aspects of all experience.
4. *The principle of self-appreciation:* Focus on the best in yourself.
5. *The principle of appreciative thought and language:* Tell a better-feeling — but believable — story.
6. *The principle of constructive response to adversity:* Recognize the advantages to be found in difficulty, misfortune, and crisis.
7. *The principle of inspired action:* Reach for a positive feeling before you act.
8. *The principle of self-empowerment in relationships:* Love others by loving yourself.

The Art of Fulfillment

Although this book is based on the science of happiness, it recognizes that happiness, at its most basic level, is an art. Science can say nothing definitive about individual capability, about you as a possible exception to the rule. Science tells us much about what most people do under normal circumstances, but it tells us almost nothing about those who break the mold, lie outside the mean, and serve as examples of what is truly possible in this world. So while I lay out principles supported by scientific research, please realize that you should customize them for yourself and your own needs.

Art is self-expression at its best. The more complicated and restricted the method, the less opportunity for self-expression and creative license. Remember, you are expressing the principles, not doing the principles. If you find yourself unhappy, your response should not be to do what it says in the fifth paragraph of the second section in a specific chapter of this book or some other "rule" book. Instead, with the eight principles in mind, you should simply move with little to no deliberation. With time, practicing the principles will become as easy, effortless, and natural as catching a ball or throwing a Frisbee.

A person who sticks tightly to a set pattern or approach to life surrenders her freedom. She comes to believe that this way is *the* way. The way of happiness is never based on one approach or one way but, instead, constantly changes form and style from moment to moment.

Happiness is a particularly personal journey and no amount of data or research can tell you what will bring you happiness. Only you can determine what will make you happier, not an "expert" in science, religion, philosophy, spirituality, or any other discipline or field. You are the expert on you!

As you read on, please keep this in mind. Practice the principles as you see fit but remember that the only person who holds the key to unlock your happy potential and your innate joy is you. Happiness is a creative expression of each individual soul. I no more hold the way for you than anybody else. I offer *one* way, one that is constantly changing, growing, and evolving. I hope it will be of immense benefit for you.

Stay fluid and master your own way. That's what happiness from the inside out is all about. And remember: The purpose of your life is happiness. The conscious decision to seek happiness in a systematic manner can profoundly change your life forever.

A CAVEAT

Before proceeding with the rest of this book, please go to the website www.authentichappiness.org and take the CES-D Questionnaire. If you fall in the "depressed" range, please follow the recommendations there and seek out licensed professional resources in your area.

1

My Life Is My Message

Discontent is the first step in progress. No one knows what is in him till he tries, and many would never try if they were not forced to.

— BASIL W. MATURIN

For too long, I was unhappy. I grew up painfully shy. In fact, I was voted "Most Shy" of my high school class. It may be hard to believe considering how much time I've spent on television screens and in front of audiences as a speaker, fashion model, actor, and corporate consultant, but it's true.

My mother, a homemaker, and my father, a computer analyst, raised my brother, my sister, and me in a humble home in western Pennsylvania. Like many married couples, my mother and father experienced their fair share of challenges. But they always weathered them. My father was the breadwinner and disciplinarian, and my mother was the caregiver. Raising three children and supporting two adults on one salary was financially stressful for both of them. Somehow, however, my siblings and I grew up to be stand-out students, above-average athletes, and well-meaning adults (most of the time, anyway). We were lovingly guided and cared for in ways some children never know.

In fact, one of the things that I remember most fondly is how my parents never seemed to miss a single game, athletic contest, concert, or school play of ours all the way through high school. Wow. I can barely take care of myself, so I sure don't know how they did all of that. On one occasion, I remember, all three of us children had a baseball or softball game on the same day. And my mother and father somehow found a way to catch several innings of each of our games. And this was before the days of digital communication, so they weren't able to be there virtually.

Despite my loving family, I found myself consistently unhappy in intangible and indescribable ways. Even at a young age, life seemed like a lot of hard work for little or no reward and hardly any lasting satisfaction at all. In the classroom, on the football field, baseball diamond, basketball court, or track, I worked myself to the bone. I studied and rewrote class notes, lifted weights for hours, shoveled snow, practiced jump shots over and over again in the freezing cold, ran wind sprints we called "suicides," and fielded ground balls until my back hurt. And despite all of my hard work and all the money my parents spent, I never felt as if I got good-enough grades, scored enough points, threw enough touchdown passes, ran fast enough, or hit enough home runs. My social life, too, was dismal. I had maybe two close friends and no girlfriend at all until I was about twenty years old.

There's Nothing Fashionable about Being Miserable

My depression took on a more philosophical nature in college. I thought my melancholy made me look intelligent, believe it or not. I embraced it — at first. I read all of the classic philosophers. I even wore this really dorky pair of glasses. Boy, I cringe now just thinking about them.

Eventually, I tired of philosophy and the facade. I genuinely wanted to feel better. I stopped reading so much philosophy. I wanted proven answers based in science, not more questions. Psychology seemed more promising in this respect. (Sorry, Professor Raff!)

Interestingly enough, after months of study, I convinced myself that I was clinically depressed. I observed all of the associated symptoms: persistently sad mood, hopelessness and pessimism, feelings of worthlessness and helplessness, loss of interest or pleasure in hobbies and activities that were once enjoyable, oversleeping, overeating, fatigue, regular thoughts of death and suicide, irritability, extreme difficulty concentrating and making even the most trivial of decisions, and persistent physical symptoms that would not respond to treatment, including back pain and digestive disorders.

In an attempt to accurately self-diagnose my depression (a fool's game!), I completed all of the self-assessments I could find. I never saw a psychiatrist, psychologist, or doctor about it. I thought they could do little to help. Later, when I watched the Woody Allen movie *Anything Else*, I was rather amused by Christina Ricci's reason for not seeing a therapist: "Jerry, I told you that psychiatrists don't work for me. I know how to trick them!" That was how I saw my depression. It was something that was logically sound and experientially proven. Everything either was bad now or would be bad soon, would forever be bad on all occasions and in all places, and there was little, if anything, I could do about any of it. That is precisely what I thought. That is precisely how I lived.

Even years later, while things on the outside changed — I had a beautiful, intelligent girlfriend, a well-paying job as a management consultant, a luxury apartment, a new BMW, a loving and supportive family, great friends, and an otherwise promising future — things on the inside seemed to only be getting worse. I knew that, inevitably, I would lose my job, experience financial ruin, break up with my girlfriend, argue with family members, disappoint friends, and lose much of everything I cared about. And it turned out that I was right. It all happened just as I had predicted, just not in that particular order. It's interesting how thoughts shape circumstance. Perhaps life really can only be understood backward and lived forward.

A Thought Saved My Life

I contemplated suicide often. To be honest, those thoughts of suicide brought me some solace. In fact, it was the realization of the solace of those thoughts that turned out to be the defining moment in my life.

One day, soon after this realization, I came to the very resolute conclusion that I would either kill myself or "fix" myself. I could not afford to risk a great job by seeking out psychiatric help. I was afraid of the stigma and the repercussions of doing so. Moreover, I figured that once the shrink realized that talking would do little good, he or she would prescribe antidepressant drugs. And I simply did not want to live that way. I had made that decision a long time before then.

Of course, my religious and spiritual beliefs — or rather, the religious and spiritual beliefs I had inherited from others — complicated issues even further. I found myself caught between the Christian belief that I would be sent to hell for taking my own life and a newly developed karmic/Buddhist philosophy that suggested I would be reincarnated right back into the same metaphysical challenge I was currently experiencing, perhaps even in a less able body and mind.

Furthermore — and this was the real catalyst for my decision — I contemplated the solace that the thought of killing myself brought. "Wow," I thought, "how interesting it is that a simple thought, notion, or idea could change my mood so quickly. If only I could master that power. Maybe it would not be 'reality' that I would be living, but who really cares if it actually works?"

And so, left with the only real, actionable alternative I could find, I proceeded to throw myself passionately into self-help books, studies on cognitive therapy, psychocybernetics, and so on. Continuing in the same vein, I matriculated and graduated years later from the Master of Applied Positive Psychology (MAPP) program at the University of Pennsylvania.

Ever since I made that decision many years ago — to make happiness my career, the principal pursuit of my life — my life has not been the same. I've been happier on a more consistent basis. When my happiness does dip, I'm usually able to quickly reestablish my original level of happiness. Previously, I lived most of my life in the lower decks of my happiness range. Now, I spend most of my life in the upper decks.

When I made the conscious decision to make happiness my dominant intent, I suddenly felt the freedom to do things I would never have done before. Here are just a few of the things I did that seemed to make a huge difference:

- I broke off an unhappy relationship with a wonderful woman for whom I was not a good fit.
- I moved to a city that was a better fit for me. (My mantra those days was "I want to live where others only vacation.") That city was Miami. I loved the sun, the fun, the beach, the playful and laid-back attitude, the diversity of the population, and the pleasant lifestyle.
- I chose a better profession for myself. (Truth be told, I was laid off. It turned out to be one of the best things that ever happened to me. I didn't know it at the time but it set the tone for the rest of my life.)
- I sold both my cars. That was a tough one because I loved my cars (a BMW and a Mercedes), but in truth

I couldn't afford them anymore. I replaced them with a scooter. To this day, I think of my scooter as one of the best purchases I've ever made.

- I rented a simple studio apartment with simple appliances and furniture in a great, convenient location. I'm a minimalist so I really felt better about doing this.

- I gave away a lot of the clothes I no longer wanted or wore.

- I spent more time outside.

- I started exercising much more and I did it outside as much as possible.

- I started eating better. This was easy and fun because I now had the time to plan my meals and I was more body conscious in this city of warm weather and scant clothing.

- I started doing things on my own, without requiring other people or circumstances to bend to my wishes or to be different in order for me to do what I wanted to do. Since I had a genuine interest in the city and since I was feeling better about myself, it was easy to do things on my own. Plus, since I didn't know anybody there, it was up to me and only me to meet new people and find my way around.

- I tried things I had never tried before. I became a huge fan of Cuban food and worked on realizing my dream of being a model and actor.

- I cut up all my credit cards and started living on cash. (Truth be told, my credit cards were maxed out and I had no choice.)

- I read a lot more, especially books about psychology and spirituality.
- I reduced my work commute significantly. Since I was splitting my time between working from home as a happiness coach and going to local modeling and acting gigs, reducing my commute was easy.
- I started writing this book.

If you'd asked me then, I honestly wouldn't have been able to explain to you why I was doing what I was doing. All I knew was that I had been unhappy for too long. I knew that what I had been doing up to that point was not working and wasn't making me feel good, either. So I changed my strategy. As the saying goes, if you keep doing what you've always done, you'll keep getting what you've always gotten.

A Thought Can Change Your Life, Too

Once I turned my life around, I vowed to help other people do the same. Your situation may not be as bad as mine was. You may not be depressed at all, much less suicidal. But you can always be happier. In the chapters to follow, I will share some of my most basic ideas about happiness. Use what works; lose what doesn't.

As you read, however, have faith and believe. Yes, I'm asking you to believe. Not just in my ability to bring about real change in your life, but in *your* ability to do so.

~:~

INSIDE-OUT HAPPINESS HABITS

✓ *Make happiness the most important pursuit of your life.*
Prioritize feeling good above all else. Make joy your
guiding principle.

✓ *Make learning more about the art and science of happiness a lifelong goal.* The first step in becoming happier
is learning about happiness, and reading the next ten
chapters is a great way to do that.

2

Authentic Happiness

Money may be the husk of many things, but not the kernel. It brings you food, but not appetite; medicine, but not health; acquaintances, but not friends; servants, but not loyalty; days of joy, but not peace or happiness.

— HENRIK·IBSEN

Scientists have reduced happiness to a simple formula. The amount and quality of happiness you experience, they say, is a function of how three different factors interact: your genetic set point for happiness, the circumstances of your life, and the things you can do voluntarily to feel happier. Written as an actual formula, it looks like this:

H (happiness) = S (genetic set point) + C (circumstances of your life) + V (voluntary factors)

This formula makes a good starting point for a discussion about the ways people go about looking for happiness and why most of those ways don't work.

The Genetic Lottery

Happiness is one of the most heritable aspects of personality. Scientists have found that between 50 and 80 percent of the variance in the average level of happiness among people can be explained by differences in their genes. In other words, some people are just born happier. They've hit the genetic lottery when it comes to happiness. They have more responsive "happy centers" in their brains. Maybe you know people like that — always smiling and looking at the bright side no matter what happens.

DNA is not destiny, however. Just because the number of happy centers in your brain is fixed does not mean that the amount of happiness you can experience in your life is fixed, too. Not at all! Becoming happier is not like becoming taller. You can become happier, in spite of a less-than-ideal genetic set point for happiness, by learning to live in the upper decks or upper levels of your happiness range more often and for longer periods of time. You can learn to play the cards that genetics has dealt you and actually improve your hand, as we will see later in this chapter.

Life Circumstances

The conditions and circumstances of your life (C in the formula) include things such as marital status, wealth, race, and gender. Obviously, characteristics like race and gender can't be changed, at least not easily. And age changes continuously whether you like it or not. Other circumstances, however, are to some extent under an individual's control. These include wealth, educational level, social status, and the place where you live. You can think of many of these things as "successful life outcomes" because we usually associate them with being successful, in one respect or another. Changing these mutable circumstances is, in fact, the major focus of many people's lives. Seeking greater wealth, status, and educational attainment is all well and good, but the verdict from the scientists of happiness is clear: by themselves, positive changes in a person's life circumstances don't lead to lasting happiness.

Empirically speaking, few, if any, external circumstances have the ability to make us lastingly happier. Science has found, for instance, that once basic needs are met, wealth and material possessions contribute less to life satisfaction than you'd predict. What this means is that hitting the lottery, being rich, buying expensive clothes, cars, and jewelry, and living a life of luxury and leisure does not guarantee happiness. Although those things might make you feel a temporary high, they won't necessarily make you lastingly happier.

It's not that money doesn't buy happiness; it can, to some extent. That's why *C* is in the happiness formula. Money buys status, freedom, and some degree of control over the circumstances of your work and life. Having these things is certainly a better basis for happiness than not having them. The problem is that while money does help people be happier than they would be without money, wealth is not by itself a sufficient condition for lasting and authentic happiness.

What's worse, when you act as if money is necessary for your happiness, you risk getting into a vicious, happiness-destroying circle. It starts with a simple relationship: the more you want relative to what you have, the unhappier you will tend to be. This can be expressed in an equation:

Happiness = What You Have (attainments) / What You Want (aspirations)

You are striving for the equation to equal 1.0 or more. If, for instance, you take home $100,000 a year but aspire to make $200,000 a year, your happiness quotient comes out like this:

$$H_1 = \$100k / \$200k = 0.5 \text{ (unhappiness)}$$

If, on the other hand, you make $80,000 a year but feel that you need an income of only $40,000, your happiness quotient is much larger:

$$H_2 = \$80k / \$40k = 2.0 \text{ (happiness)}$$

Even though in this latter case you make less than in the first scenario, you are likely much happier because of the simple fact that your aspirations are set much lower.

The reason this can lead to a vicious circle of unhappiness is that aspirations tend to overwhelm reality when you chase financial success. The more you make, the more you become convinced you need to make, or should make. As a result, your happiness quotient drops below the break-even point of 1.0 and keeps dropping.

In other words, no matter how much money you make, you always want more and therefore feel poor. For this reason, the amount of money a person makes only approximately and moderately predicts his or her level of happiness. Rising desires for goods and services serve to cancel the effects of greater income for many people. So, in short, it's good to have money, of course, but bad to want it too much. Regardless of your actual income, it's your material aspirations that determine whether you're happy with that income.

The other reason that money doesn't guarantee happiness is that making more money often means working more hours, hours that might otherwise be spent in more highly rewarding and happiness-producing activities, such as spending time with family or friends. It is for these reasons, among others, that some of the richest people are actually the most miserable and some of the poorest people are, ironically, the happiest.

Other external circumstances also have little to no effect on happiness levels. Educational level doesn't affect happiness at all. Marriage is associated with happiness, but that's mostly because people who get married are generally happier to begin with. The climate in which they live doesn't impact happiness for most people, either, despite what almost all people think. And although having a child does tend to make women happier, it doesn't have that effect on men. Furthermore, having additional children beyond the firstborn actually lowers the happiness of both parents. In fact, parents' happiness hits a low point when their children reach the teenage years, and marital satisfaction starts heading back up again only when the kids leave home. Of course — and this is important to note — these effects will not hold true for everyone on all occasions. These statistics speak only to the majority of people on most occasions. Some people will find children greatly rewarding and their happiness ratings will soar as a result.

There's a great Michael Bay–directed movie I once watched called *The Island*, starring Ewan McGregor and Scarlett Johansson. The movie takes place in 2019. According to the premise, most of the outside world has been contaminated and a community of people have been rescued from the toxic outside world to live in a controlled environment. The rules of living are selected for them; clothing, meals, leisure, and jobs are all structured and controlled. Everyone in the community anticipates a special event every week — the lottery — in which one new person wins a chance to move to a tropical paradise, the only uncontaminated natural area left on Earth, known as "The Island."

This premise — the possibility of moving to a real tropical island where you can live happily ever after — makes for a great movie plot, but it's a terrible basis for living your life. And yet, how many of us live just like this, believing the bad news we hear every day and the stories that the world we live in is an unhappy, hopeless place? Are you waiting for just the right circumstances to fall out of the sky — waiting to be handpicked to join the other lucky guests in some pristine utopia and live happily ever after? Well, it doesn't happen that way. Even in the movie it doesn't go that way. As .it turns out, the world isn't contaminated at all and the island is made up. It doesn't exist. And the "lucky few" who win the lottery and are selected to move to the nonexistent island to live happily ever after actually end up serving as organ donors for the wealthy. In a metaphorical sense, they become the sacrificial lambs of the rich and successful.

Most people will live out their entire lives and never truly understand the source of their unhappiness or discontent. They will live a lifetime — seventy, eighty, or ninety years or more — and never really get it. They will live out their entire lives believing that if they had only taken that job, met that man, married that woman, won that race, tried harder, been more beautiful, worked longer hours, or moved to that made-up tropical paradise, they'd have achieved success and that success would have brought them happiness. They will have lived their entire lives playing by the wrong rules.

The Controllable Causes of Happiness

The most important factors to focus on for becoming happier, then, are the voluntary factors (V in the formula). These factors include your daily behaviors and your state of mind, or consciousness. They are the most important factors because they are the most immediately changeable and have the greatest impact on happiness. They are also important because they hold the key to changing, in a positive way, the C in your happiness equation — your life circumstances.

Happiness is an incredibly personal and case-specific venture. The truth is that your happiness is determined more by your state of mind than by the external circumstances of your life. *A happy person is not a person in a certain set of circumstances but, rather, a person with a certain set of attitudes.* The happiness of your life depends on the quality of the thoughts in your head, not the quantity of dollars in your pocket, the number of children you have at home, or the diplomas you have in your office. If you are not happy, you have to change your attitude.

Since the beginning of time, people have been trying to change the world so that they can be happy. This has never worked. It's backward. It's like seeing a blurry spot on a photograph and trying to remove it by rubbing the photograph instead of cleaning the smudge on the camera lens. It is just as futile to think we can change people or the world as it is to rub a photograph to "erase" a flaw caused by something on the lens. When you realize that the problem is on the camera lens, you can clear the lens itself. You work with thoughts or causes, not outcomes or effects. You don't change behavior, only the consciousness that creates it.

Synthetic Happiness

Most of us have an intuitive sense, at least, that happiness is an inside job — that it comes more from attitudes than from external circumstances. And yet, we still focus all our energy on the pursuit of success and expect that to make us happy. Why do we do this? If what we are doing isn't making us happy, why do we continue doing it anyway?

Well, there are two reasons why we do this. First, trying to buy happiness with success is initially more seductive. Success is more tangible, more visible. And the media glamorize it. Truth be told, success is easier to advertise and sell than happiness.

Here's a good example of what I mean. Recently, I've been shopping a happiness-flavored television show. It's a good one. I met with the head of a major network, a network known for its softly educational but entertaining bent. After I pitched the idea, the head of programming turned to me and said, "Wow. Now that's a phenomenal show! The only problem is that it's hard to show happiness on a television screen. It doesn't translate well. How can we show that somebody is feeling better, feeling happier, without showing cars, clothes, partying, and sex?"

The second reason people try to buy happiness with success is that they actually mistake success for happiness. They think success and happiness are the same thing, or at least *should* be the same thing. But happiness is more than success. In fact, I'd go so far as to say that too single-minded a pursuit of success gets in the way of your happiness. Pursuing success for its own sake is like trying to synthesize happiness. It's more expensive than growing it naturally and it's worse for you, too.

The Pursuit of Unhappiness

The pursuit of success is actually a thinly veiled pursuit of unhappiness. If you believe that your happiness depends on being successful, then it follows that *un*happiness can be cured by being more successful. So, the unhappier you are about your current situation, the more resolutely you pursue success. And to try to prove to yourself that this strategy is working, you also seek pleasure, which — for short periods of time, at least — feels like happiness. But because happiness equals pleasure *and* meaning, your unhappiness only grows. And the more your unhappiness grows, the more you chase the false goals of success and pleasure. In that chase, as you prioritize success and pleasure above all else, you plant and nurture the same seeds of discontent that had you chasing success and pleasure in the first place. And this discontent incites a more aggressive pursuit of success and pleasure in the hope that it will bring happiness. The unhappiness that results from this pursuit will spur on even more valiant attempts at achieving success and satisfying desire and so on and so on. Life may bring rewards but less and less lasting peace or satisfaction.

Does it now make sense why, despite things being so objectively good for many of us, we don't seem to be feeling much better for it? We've created a giant vicious circle: Discontent drives the rat race and hedonism; and the rat race and hedonism create more discontent. The unhappier you are about your situation, the more you try to improve it by stepping up the pace in the rat race. And the more you fail to achieve happiness this way, the unhappier you are about your situation.

For most people, giving up on success is a hard pill to swallow. The pursuit of success seems so promising. Success is seriously seductive. Pleasure is oh so sexy. Nature has designed us to feel this way. Evolutionarily speaking, success, status, and pleasure mattered more to our ancestors than happiness because a pursuit of success and status meant survival for our ancestors and their children and their children's children. Happiness took a backseat to survival. Now, with many of us living above the most primitive levels of subsistence and with new tools, resources, and support at our fingertips, unhappiness for extended periods of time isn't as easily justified; we can't blame unhappiness on the rain, so to speak. In other words, we can't blame our unhappiness on an inability to meet our basic physical needs like clothing, shelter, and food. Neither can we blame it on a lack of available expertise, guidance, technology, or other resources. All kinds of help from all kinds of sources are at our disposal.

The Unhappiness Treadmill

Two concepts help explain why successful life outcomes do not and cannot make you lastingly happier. I call them the revolving door of desire and the unhappiness treadmill. Once you understand these two concepts, you'll be able to see them in action in your own life and then work to remove yourself from their gravitational pull.

The pursuit of success doesn't make you lastingly happy because even when you get what you want, what you wanted gets old once you've gotten it. Then, in order to get the same high, you need more and more of it. There's a reason I'm comparing success and its trappings to drugs — they really do work the same way. Once you have a certain materialistic experience, you need to keep on having more of it if you want to sustain your happiness.

Things that were once new and sparkly lose that fresh, new-car scent and slowly fade, but most of us forget or underestimate this effect. You can't bottle the experience of owning something new, and you can't stop time no matter how hard you try. What used to make you happy no longer does. We expect things to make us happier for longer periods of time than they actually do or can. To get the same effect from the same thing, increasingly higher doses are required. This is the unhappiness treadmill.

The Revolving Door of Desire

The second reason why successful life outcomes don't make you lastingly happy is that what you want always changes. Happiness based on success is a moving target. What most of us don't realize is that we will always have unfulfilled or unsatisfied desires. Desire can never be satisfied once and for all. For every desire satisfied, another is created. One satisfied desire becomes the basis for the next, which, when satisfied, will become the platform for yet another. This issue is endemic to life itself. There is no escaping it. I call this phenomenon the revolving door of desire.

You live your entire life in a gap, a gap between what you want or who you have become and where you are. One of the keys to happiness, then, is to learn to appreciate the nature of desire and put it in its place. You have to learn to accept the fact that you will always be incomplete, that you will always have unfulfilled and unsatisfied desires until the day you are dead — and that this is actually a good thing. You must realize that happiness does not rest on your ability to satisfy every desire, to fulfill every longing once and for all. You can't permanently stop the revolving door of desire, so you might as well enjoy the ride.

A client of mine — let's call him Jared — called for some coaching because he quit a six-figure job to pursue an entrepreneurial opportunity in fashion with his brother. The funny thing (to me) is that he loved the job he quit. And he hated fashion. But he wanted a Ferrari and a boat and he thought he would never be able to afford either one of those things while working in investment banking, so he quit. "Rob," he told me, "I hate this fashion thing and I'm not making any money at it. I don't understand why I'm never able to be completely satisfied forever with any one thing. I don't understand what would possess me to quit a great job making great money in this economy to pursue such a terrible opportunity doing something I hate just so I can buy stuff I don't need! Why is the grass always greener?"

On average, Americans over the course of their lives move more than six times, change jobs more than ten times, and marry more than once, which suggests that most of us aren't very good at nailing down this desire thing once and for all.

Inside-Out Happiness Is Authentic Happiness

As I reflect back on my decision to make happiness my top priority, and on the actions that I took as a result, I can now see that one thing made all the difference: I stopped letting other people tell me what I wanted. I stopped letting society define my ambitions. I stopped letting family and friends dictate my desires. I will tell you the same: stop letting other people tell you what you want. Become independent of the opinions of others. Stop your endless search for approval and acceptance from others. If you don't, the only happiness you'll ever find is synthetic happiness.

Real happiness comes from spending your life in your own way. If you walk in another's shoes or take another's path, you don't leave any footprints of your own. This doesn't mean you have to be different from everyone else, and it doesn't mean that others can't offer you wisdom. It simply means learning to tell the difference between what comes from within and what is imposed on you from the outside. Happiness, you see, is nothing if it's not about being more and more of who you really are.

How much of what you think you want is what you *really* want and how much of it is something society, friends, family members, or colleagues say you *should* want? How much of it is intrinsically rewarding and how much of it is only extrinsically rewarding? How much of what you do daily is only for the benefit of show? Which things are socially conditioned? Sometimes our dreams and desires come more from our culture than from our unique, individual souls. When this is true they can be the source of much unhappiness and turmoil.

For instance, do you really want to own a home instead of renting an apartment? Do you really want to own your car instead of leasing one, get married instead of staying single (or being in an unwed but committed relationship), or work a corporate job instead of being an entrepreneur? What do you, dear reader, really want and what does society say you should want? Can you tell the difference between your wants or desires and other people's (or society's) wants or desires? Begin to tease out what society says you should want from what you really want. In fact, I'd go so far as to recommend that, above all else, you get clear on what you want by taking everybody else out of the picture. Step out of the illusion. When you really get this one day, you'll just decide to get up and get out of the movie. You'll step back into your authenticity.

You can do this by asking the infinitely regressive "why?" question: Why do you want what you want? Keep asking this question until you've peeled back all the layers of that desire and you've gotten to the core, the essence, of what you really want.

Why do you want to own that home? Is it for the tax break? Do you want to impress other people with its size? Or does having a home you can call your own reflect your core values? Why do you want to get married and have children? Is it because you love your partner unequivocally and unconditionally and know that having children is your meaning and purpose in life? Or is it because you feel incomplete, unsuccessful, or like a failure relative to your friends who are married and have children? Are there ways to meet these same needs or desires in more productive and efficient ways?

Question some of the assumptions that you're living and working under. Question your motives. Get to the root of them. Identify and execute against your own goals. Claim and live your own life. You're not here on this planet or in this world to live somebody else's life.

This may or may not mean giving up the rat race and the

pleasure chase. Either way, however, it will mean learning to exchange synthetic happiness — the temporary high that comes from success and pleasure — for authentic happiness, the more lasting sense of satisfaction that comes from a life full of pleasure *and* meaning. It will mean learning to stop trying to synthesize happiness from material ingredients.

As you reflect back on your life, look forward to the future state of your own affairs, and plan for happiness, I would strongly encourage you to ask yourself four incredible questions:

1. Is this what I want or what somebody else wants?
2. Is this what I want or what somebody else wants for me?
3. Is this what I want or what I want for somebody else?
4. Does this feel like authentic happiness or synthetic happiness?

Consider the words of Charles Kingsley: "We act as though comfort and luxury were the chief requirements of life, when all that we need to make us really happy is something to be enthusiastic about." What are you uniquely enthusiastic about?

Happiness: The Master Key to Success

Once you give up trying to make success your path to happiness and instead decide to make happiness itself your goal, you are more likely to be successful. How's that for sweet irony? Over a decade of research shows that successful people, by and large, are happy first. Happiness comes before, and leads to, success. Happy people — those who experience a preponderance of positive emotions — are more successful and accomplished in all areas of their lives, including their career, their relationships, and their health. Happiness, then, is not only the greatest form of success; it is also its root.

Happy people are more successful professionally. They secure more job interviews, are evaluated more positively by supervisors once they obtain a job, show superior performance and productivity, and handle managerial roles better. They show more effective workplace behavior and hold jobs longer. Finally, happy individuals also make more money.

Happy people are more successful socially and romantically. They are more likely than their less happy peers to have fulfilling marriages and relationships. Love, friendship, and positive social relationships are most likely to be created when people are in a positive mood and their perspectives are more expansive, tolerant, and creative. Not only does happiness protect against pain and inspire us to take more health and safety precautions, but positive emotions even undo negative emotions.

Happy people are healthier and live longer. Optimism predicts better health because an optimistic explanatory style calms and quiets the immune system, encourages a person to seek medical advice and to stick to health regimens, keeps the number of actual bad life events low, and encourages deeper friendships and love.

Truly, if there ever were a law of attraction in action, this would be it. To be successful in any area of your life, to change the conditions and circumstances of your life, you must get happy first. In other words, when you get happy, you live your life in the rainbow. And at the end of the rainbow is that pot of gold. Finding the pot of gold without taking the path laid out by the rainbow is an impossible mission.

As it turns out, reality — for happy people — is much sweeter than fantasy. Science has strong data to support that. Anybody can learn to be happier and thus wealthier and healthier. You don't need to have the right friends and the right connections, get the right education, live in the right city, look the right way, be the right age, work in the right field or industry, or make more money. You simply have to do what you can with what you have from where you are.

This may not be news to you. Yet, you still might have trouble putting your happiness first. You might still find it difficult to prioritize happiness over success. If so, remember the simple words of W. L. Bateman: "If you keep on doing what you've always done, you'll keep on getting what you've always got."

A New Approach

One of my favorite Seinfeld television episodes is called "The Opposite." George, on visiting the beach, decides that every decision he has ever made has been wrong, and that his life is the exact opposite of what it should be. Later, at Monk's Café with the gang, he tells Jerry about his revelation. "I had so much promise," he says. "I was personable, I was bright. Oh, maybe not academically speaking, but . . . I was perceptive. I always know when someone's uncomfortable at a party. It became very clear to me sitting out there today that every decision I've ever made, in my entire life, has been wrong. My life is the opposite of everything I want it to be. Every instinct I have, in every area of life, be it something to wear, something to eat. . . . It's all been wrong."

Jerry listens and reasons, "If every instinct you have is wrong, then the opposite would have to be right." George then resolves to start doing the complete opposite of what he would do normally.

In one particularly funny scene, George meets an attractive woman. Normally, in this situation, he would never dare approach her. But since he's living this principle of opposites, he decides he has to introduce himself to her. "Excuse me, I couldn't help but notice that you were looking in my direction. My name is George. I'm unemployed and I live with my parents." Her response is surprisingly positive. She later becomes his girlfriend.

By doing the opposite of what he's always done, he suddenly and almost miraculously begins to experience good luck. In addition to finding a girlfriend, he moves out of his parents' house and even lands a job with the New York Yankees. How's that for results?

Well, I was George Costanza in some small way (except my grades were better and I was a six-foot-three-inch black man). After a moment of realization, I started doing the opposite of what I had always done. I started doing what I wanted to do and what made me feel good. And it actually worked!

Interestingly enough, most of us are like George. Intuitively, we know what would make us happier. Sometimes it's embarrassingly elementary. It's just a matter of changing course and doing things differently. Unlike George, we don't have to do the exact opposite of everything we'd normally do. Some of our habits and instincts are good ones. But many of us need to shake up our lives pretty radically by starting to do the things we know will make us happier (and healthier).

Don't know where to start? Here's a list from Barry Schwartz's book *The Paradox of Choice*: Spend more time with family and friends. Take longer vacations, even if that means making less money. Exercise more, eat better, sleep more, and spend more time outdoors. Reduce your commuting time, even if it means living in a smaller house. Choose a career you love that's a good fit for your personality and strengths, even if it means earning less. Use cash instead of credit. Buy basic, functional appliances, furniture, and cars. Invest the money you save. All these things have been proven to make people happier.

So, what are you going to do differently?

⌁:∿

INSIDE-OUT HAPPINESS HABITS

✓ *Stop trying to synthesize happiness.* Give up your single-minded pursuit of success. Choose to grow authentic happiness, instead. It's cheaper and better for you.

✓ *Don't let other people or society tell you what you want.* Divorce what you want from what other people want or what other people want for you.

3

Finding Pleasure *and* Meaning

A happy life is one which is in accordance with its own nature.
— MARCUS ANNAEUS SENECA

When I was attending Swarthmore College, my dad would call every month to check on how I was doing. One call I remember very well. "So, Rob, we're spending a lot of money on this college education," he began. "Are you working hard, boy, or what?"

Always appreciating how hard my father worked to put me and my two siblings through school, I quickly responded, "Yes, Dad, of course. I'm killing myself."

He laughed heartily. "Well, stop it, you dummy! If you're working hard, you're doing something wrong. Work smart, not hard. Haven't you ever heard of 'lazy intelligence'? How do you think Bill Gates got rich? And Michael Jordan? You see how long his baseball career lasted! If you're going to work hard, work hard at the right things, and then it won't feel like such hard work."

His advice took some time to sink in, but I got it eventually. Most people try too hard at the wrong things. Most people take the path of greatest resistance, as I did in college. They think they'll be rewarded for the hard work. That might work in school, but it doesn't usually work in the real world and it doesn't work with happiness, either. When it comes to happiness, the right way is often the easy way.

It's not that hard work itself is incompatible with happiness. Sometimes the happy path requires considerable effort. What's important is that the effort and time you put into something have a proportional payoff in greater happiness. That may sound obvious, but it's amazing how many people have very little idea of what really makes them happy and act as if hard work is an end in itself. They put too much time and energy into things that don't make them happy.

When life seems like a constant struggle, it may be a sign that you're not investing your time and energy wisely in things that bring you the most fulfillment and satisfaction. When you know what makes you happy and you invest your time and energy appropriately, life flows effortlessly. It feels like you're taking the path of least resistance.

Your Happiness Islands

Before you can begin investing your time and energy in what's going to bring you the most happiness, you have to know what makes you happy. This may not be as easy as it sounds. One problem is that we've internalized all those external definitions of what it means to be happy and what should bring us happiness. In addition, happiness is complex — it involves, as you'll recall, both pleasure and meaning.

Think back to the times in your life when you have been really happy, when you have been sublimely heady or, at least, unusually happy. What were you doing at those times? What did these activities have in common? Who was involved? When has your life been brimming with enthusiasm, excitement, and well-being? Think about the activities, or kinds of activities, that evoke the most natural, effortless, and frequent feelings of felicity. Look for themes. These are your happiness islands.

Now think back to the times in your life when you have been unusually successful, when you have achieved important things. Think back to your peak performances. When did they take place? With whom did they take place? What kinds of activities were involved? What comes more quickly, effortlessly, and naturally to you than anything else? Look for themes. All this will point to your natural strengths. Doing things in which you can apply your strengths gives you a sense of meaning and purpose. These activities are what I call your achievement islands.

Look for overlap between your achievement islands and your happiness islands. What activities come naturally, exercise your strengths, *and* bring you great satisfaction? This is where happiness lives for you. Find these islands and live on them as much as you can. Think about how you can spend more time and energy on these activities and thereby squeeze more juice from those most fruitful endeavors.

I love reading, running and working out, listening to music, attending inspirational seminars and workshops, reading books on psychology, philosophy, and spirituality, watching funny movies, spending time at the pool or beach, and coaching people who've solicited my advice. For the time and effort invested, these activities really bring me a lot of happiness. They are my happiness islands. And among these activities, attending inspirational seminars and workshops and reading books on psychology, philosophy, and spirituality are effortless activities that play to my natural strengths; they are my achievement islands. Engaged in those activities, I'm able to reach uncommon levels of happiness and unparalleled levels of success or achievement relative to other activities.

Now, consider your "desert" islands in terms of achievement. What activities and tasks do you always seem to struggle with? What do most of your peers seem to do more easily, more quickly, and more naturally than you? This may be a hard one if you're good at many different things. So think about those times when you've invested a lot of time, energy, and effort and reaped less reward than you might have expected.

Next, consider your unhappiness islands — your desert islands for happiness. What activities or tasks bring you more pain, frustration, disappointment, or disgust than any others? When have you been at your lowest, bluest, or darkest hour? With what people and in what capacity were you involved? Look for themes.

Again, look for overlap. Where do you achieve the least and invite the most unhappiness, too? What activities are most unrewarding both from an emotional perspective and from a material perspective? Find them and then get rid of as many of them as quickly as humanly possible.

For example, I hate talking on the phone at length, responding to emails, traveling in any form, managing my finances, managing a blog, partying extra late, drinking too much, running marathons or decathlons, eating too much, doing favors that people can do for themselves, and watching the news and television. They are very low-value activities for me. They make me feel drained and uninspired, and they bring me very little, if any, happiness or success. These are my unhappiness islands.

Once you identify what brings you fulfillment and allows you to apply your natural strengths as much as possible every day at work and at play, you can think about how you can spend more time exploiting your best, most profitable resources. You can learn how to spend more time on your happiness islands and less time on your unhappiness islands. Then, the vacation you seek will be the life you have.

Find your natural strengths or talents so that you can exploit them. Go to www.authentichappiness.org and take the VIA Strengths Questionnaire. The assessment will identify your top five strengths. Look for ways to use your top two or three strengths every day at work and at play.

Happiness Profit

As you may have noticed, not everything in life offers the same kind of value to you, and what's most valuable is usually only a very small subset of the whole. This is why you probably wear a minority of your clothes a majority of the time, why a small portion of what you do daily at work is responsible for a large portion of the enjoyment and recognition you get from your job, and why you spend most of your time with a few select individuals who bring you the most pleasure. A few things in life pay huge dividends, and most things just don't.

This principle is especially important when it comes to happiness. You can put the same amount of effort or time into different activities but net completely different results in terms of happiness or satisfaction. It depends on the activity you pursue, the people involved, and the approach you take. If you think about it, a lot of what you do probably brings you very little happiness for the time and energy invested, while certain other things you do bring you lots of happiness for the small amount of time or energy invested.

If you are like most people, you probably spend the majority of your time and energy on the low-satisfaction activities and only a small amount of your time and energy on a select few high-satisfaction activities. If happiness is your ultimate goal, that's not a wise use of your time and energy.

So, look closely at how you use your time and energy, using happiness as your measuring stick. I spend my time trying to get the most happiness bang for my energy buck. I look for those things that give me the biggest reward, happinesswise, for the least amount of effort. That's what smart people do. And that's what happy people do, too.

Now, if you follow this advice, you'll soon find out that even though it works very well, there's a limit to the happiness you can squeeze out of any particular activity. As you increase the amount of time spent at your high-happiness-value activities, you begin to experience what's called diminishing marginal utility. That is, each additional hour or day you spend pursuing that activity will, at some critical threshold, become less and less rewarding. But as long as you remember that it's all about maximizing happiness "profit," you can deal with this problem in a way that allows you to get more done and leaves you feeling oh so much happier at the same time.

Within each of your happiness islands, figure out the location of that critical threshold where your happiness profit begins to diminish. You can tell when you pass this balance point by staying attuned to how you feel as you spend time in your activities. As long as you feel inspired, strong, and energized, keep going. When you find yourself feeling drained, tired, weak, and uninspired, stop. If you dread the thought of doing something or don't have enthusiasm for it, it's a sign you've already milked as much fulfillment from it as you're going to get. It's that simple. As you spend more and more time paying attention to your internal happiness gauge, you'll get better and better at identifying exactly when you've maximized your happiness profit within a certain activity.

For instance, in my own life, I've found that I accrue the most benefit and the least detriment working out forty-five minutes a day five to six days a week. Anything more than that and I begin to dread the gym. Anything less than that and I feel like I'm not doing enough; I feel like more happiness juice can still be squeezed out of that happiness-producing activity.

The point isn't to become an exercise addict, sex addict, or shopping addict. Likewise, the point isn't to become a beach bum, couch potato, or vagabond. The point is to find the right portfolio of activities that gives you the most benefit for the least effort, cost, or pain. For many activities, you may be already going beyond the point where more effort brings more happiness, so you will need to scale back these activities. For other things, it may feel as though that threshold doesn't exist at all and you stop only because you have to. Find that place where you maximize happiness profit and stay there.

"Good Enough" Decision Making

The principle of smart energy investment applies equally well to making decisions. One of the things you can do to get happy is to learn when you have invested enough time and energy in a decision. Many people put far too much effort into making decisions, creating anxiety and stress. And then the decisions they make don't necessarily make them any happier. The secret to avoiding this trap is to stop at good enough. This means that not only do you stop trying to make the perfect decision every time, but you put the whole decision-making process in perspective, realizing that few decisions are really all that momentous and that agonizing over them only detracts from your goal of being happy.

Before I understood this principle of "good enough," I would spend hours in the Targets, Walmarts, and CostCos of the world. It was nearly impossible for me to make a decision on any particular product without comparing all of the necessary ingredients, features, or aspects of each competing item. If I was shopping for shampoo, I had to read the list of ingredients for each brand. As if that wasn't enough, I had to check the prices and the unit prices, too, to make sure I was getting the best bargain. And I couldn't just go through this process once, decide on a shampoo, and then purchase that same brand and size of shampoo on every visit to the store. No. I had to begin the process all over again each time I went to the store. After all, perhaps there was a new and improved product, something I hadn't heard of or tried before. Or perhaps there was a sale that week. I just couldn't live thinking that I may have missed an opportunity to buy a better product at a cheaper price. Never mind that I really didn't have any hair.

If that wasn't bad enough, I'd go through this process for every single product I purchased, from toiletries to dinners out. It was overwhelming and it brought me more anxiety and stress than I wanted. Why was I wasting so much time, effort, and energy making what most people consider such trivial choices? Eventually, I figured out how to handle it. I decided what I was in the mood for and what I wanted to get out of something before I went to that store, that restaurant, that car dealership, or that social gathering. I didn't necessarily write it all out but I was clear about what the main purpose or goal of going was: to feel good.

When I remembered that going to the store wasn't about getting the best shampoo, going to the restaurant wasn't about getting the best entrée, going to the car dealership wasn't about getting the best deal, and going to the social gathering or party wasn't about meeting the prettiest, most intelligent woman, my anxiety faded fast. When I remembered that going to the store was about being as efficient as possible in providing for my material needs, that going to the restaurant was about enjoying the stress-free company of my friends and family, and that going to the party was about meeting new and interesting people who could add something of value to my life, I began finding a lot more happiness in all my decisions and all my activities. I had a better time and I was happier with the decisions I made. I built less expectation into them. I stopped at good enough. I let the latest and greatest and new and improved goods, services, events, and people find me.

My friend and former professor Barry Schwartz explains this approach to decision making in his book *The Paradox of Choice*. If you establish criteria, or set and clarify your top, most important goals or intentions before you look at the options available, says Schwartz, you will find that your life is a lot better off for it. Decide what you really value before you go out into the world and look at all of the choices. And then stop when those criteria have been met or that intention or those goals have been achieved. By doing so, you will eliminate the stress, anxiety, anticipated regret, indecision, and invested effort that often come from making a decision. Science tells us that the more time you spend trying to make a decision, the less happy you will be with whatever decision you make.

"Good enough" doesn't mean you can't have high standards. Learning to stop at "good enough" just means that you realize that an objectively good decision is only beneficial to the extent that it's also a subjectively good decision. At some point, too much time and effort invested in deciding mean no amount of return or payoff will satisfy your ballooned expectations.

The main point is that by learning to stop at "good enough," you choose decision criteria that are related to happiness and not external measures of success. Even if you don't agonize over many decisions, you could still use the wrong criteria — criteria based on impressing or pleasing other people, looking successful, being respected, building status or prestige, or boosting your ego — and make subjectively bad decisions, decisions that make you feel bad, as a result.

The Happiness Prescription

Happiness is like an eye test. When you go to the optometrist's office, the doctor sits you in front of this big machine with all these different lenses built inside. Then the doctor has you look at an eye chart on the wall while he or she flips through those lenses, one after the other, each time asking, "Better or worse . . . okay; now, better or worse . . . good; now this one or that one?" Eventually, he or she nails down your prescription. Happiness results from a similar process. It comes after a progressive series of corrective better-or-worse questions. And your job in seeking happiness is just to answer those questions honestly and accurately and then move on. Life itself plays the role of the doctor for the most part, but you can always schedule your own happiness exams at your whim and discretion, too.

Eventually, as you move toward the better-feeling activities, the better-feeling people, the better-feeling thoughts, and the better-feeling words and actions and away from their worse-feeling counterparts, your happiness prescription gets nailed down. And just like your eyes, your happiness sometimes needs a checkup to see if your prescription has changed. It's really no big deal. You just take the same test over again, answer the same questions, and are once again living with the clarity and confidence you're used to.

As we move through the principles in this book, I want you to keep this principle in mind. Take the path of greatest reward. The point isn't to suffer your way to happiness. The point isn't to see how much you can torture yourself on the way to bliss and well-being. No amount of unhappiness will ever buy you happiness no matter how hard you try. I promise you. I've tried. My clients have tried. *You've* tried! It doesn't work.

When you practice this principle of investing your energy to get the maximum happiness profit and you trust what brings better-feeling feelings, you end up spending more of your time going with the flow of life, where it's easy, and less of your time trying to paddle upstream. The ride is

much more enjoyable that way. And enjoying the ride —
pardon the cliché — is what happiness really is. What's
more, when you go with the flow, you are likely to find down-
stream all those things you want. So it's a win-win situation,
the best of both worlds.

Combining Pleasure and Meaning

As you gravitate toward the activities, people, interests, and
projects that bring you happiness, remember to keep in mind
that real happiness combines both pleasure and meaning.
Look for things that give you both, not just one or the other.
In most cases, passion points to purpose, but not always.
Sometimes, passion just points to pleasure and you have to
add some meaning to the recipe to get purpose. For instance,
going to the beach every day brings me lots of pleasure but
little to no meaning. To turn this pleasure island into a happiness island I feed it with meaning. I take a friend or a good,
meaningful book with me to the beach. I've found that
adding people or tying a pleasurable activity to a larger mission or objective helps turn almost any pleasure island into
a happiness island. Just make sure those people you bring
along make you feel better, generally, and make you feel better about yourself, especially.

In other cases, your happiness island will really feel more
like an island of meaning than one of pleasure. In those
instances, you want to look for ways to introduce more pleasure and fun into the activity. For example, writing this book
is very meaningful for me. And it's also my job. But depending on the topic, I don't always get a ton of pleasure from it.

So to introduce more pleasure into this work, I play music, add a personal story, take snack breaks, or situate myself right in front of a large window with a view of the bay. Now these things might not work for you; you have to find your own way of introducing more pleasure into your meaning, or vice versa.

Go to www.authentichappiness.org and take the Approaches to Happiness Questionnaire. The very brief assessment will help you decide whether you need to increase the pleasure or meaning in your life.

Reconciling the Present and the Future

So far I've talked mostly about operating your life in the present — making decisions about how to invest your energy smartly today. It would be nice if that were all we had to do, but the realities of life require that we also think about how our actions in the present impact our lives in the future.

People have two opposing tendencies with regard to the future. On the one hand, we seek pleasure in the moment, disregarding the consequences this may have for us later. This is what Freud called the Pleasure Principle. On the other hand, we are able to defer gratification in order to obtain longer-lasting or more assured pleasure in the future. Freud had a name for this, too — the Reality Principle.

Happiness, for me, is a comprehensive pursuit, one that takes into account both the Pleasure Principle and the Reality

Principle. It recognizes the immediacy of the present moment and also the exigencies of future moments. It's a pursuit aimed at maximizing profit by taking into account both costs and benefits. To find real happiness, you need to shy away from what brings only transitory pleasure at the expense of long-term benefit (that is, hedonism) and be equally wary of what sacrifices pleasure for hypothetical long-term benefits (that is, the single-minded pursuit of success). Look for what can bring you real benefit in both the short term and the long term.

Professor Tal Ben-Shahar at Harvard uses a great metaphor to describe how you can maximize both short-term *and* long-term benefit effectively. He calls it "the Hamburger Model." In this model, hedonism, or pleasure chasing, is like eating a fast-food hamburger every day. It tastes great but it's bad for your health and will probably shorten your life. Likewise, hedonism is not a good policy for lasting happiness. At the other end of the scale, participating in the rat race isn't a good policy for lasting happiness, either, because rat racing is like eating a soy burger every day for the rest of your life. It's good for you but it doesn't taste very good. The best policy for lasting happiness, according to Ben-Shahar, is finding a compromise between the two extremes, which he likens to eating a turkey burger. It tastes good *and* it's good for you. Now tell me that isn't a cool metaphor for an Ivy League professor!

Without knowing it, I found a way to practice Ben-Shahar's technique in my own social life. When I first moved to Miami, I was partying almost every day. And it was a blast

— at first. With time, I became worn down and never felt quite right. So, ultimately, I would retreat from the social scene for a few weeks and recuperate. Of course, that would soon get boring, so I'd then charge full-speed back into the party scene. Eventually, that back-and-forth cycle became exhausting.

I tried something different. I learned to pick my spots. I became more selective. I stopped going to clubs so much and started going to restaurants and lounges more often. I started my night earlier and ended it earlier. I stopped drinking and, when I did drink, I scaled it back to just a couple. I stopped inviting everybody out to party with me. I invited just those people with whom I had fun *and* with whom I had meaningful conversations.

Through a combination of acts, I was able to experience more pleasure overall. I got to socialize, hear great music, eat great food, and party regularly — and experience more meaning, too. I established closer, more meaningful relationships with my real friends, had more productive workdays, and didn't lose track of where my life was going. I stayed focused on my larger purpose.

As you go about your life and make decisions about what to do, keep in mind the following questions:

1. Will this decision bring me more or less pleasure? Will it bring me more or less meaning?
2. Is there a way to squeeze both more meaning and more pleasure out of this activity or decision?

3. For both the long term and the short term, how can I reap the most benefit from this activity and bear the least cost?

4. Is there a way to squeeze both short-term gain and long-term gain out of this activity or decision?

The Company Counts

One important note should be made here. Often, the way to increase both pleasure and meaning is to invite the right company — and the right company is happy company — along for the ride. If you want to have a happy life, there's nothing like surrounding yourself with happy people.

There was a time during my "new" life when I had been spending a lot of time inside my apartment working on this book. I remember feeling uncharacteristically blue and melancholy, and I couldn't explain why. My mother, the intuitive healer and genius that she is, suggested I get outside and socialize with friends for a bit. It was a simple remedy, but boy did that send my happiness soaring. Try it yourself. You'll be surprised at the pleasurable and meaningful difference it makes. Chris Peterson, one of my professors at Penn and co-author of *Character Strengths and Virtues*, used to put it oh so simply: "Relationships matter." Those relationships needn't be romantic ones. They can just as easily and profitably be platonic friendships. In fact, most of you will find that those are the most lasting relationships you'll have in your life.

The good life is really about getting both pleasure and meaning. To the extent that you can maximize pleasure and meaning in your life in both the short term and the long term while minimizing the associated effort, time, and pain, you will find happiness a much more effortless pursuit. Think in terms of the principle of investing your energy for the maximum return on happiness in every arena of your life: relationships and social life, career and work life, health and physical body, spirituality, and so on. You'll find happiness every time.

~:~

INSIDE-OUT HAPPINESS HABITS

✓ *Do more of what's already working and do less of what isn't working.* Reduce, delegate, or eliminate what doesn't bring you happiness or has too high a cost in pain or effort.

✓ *Find your natural strengths or talents and exploit them.*

✓ *Find your natural course and follow it.* Your natural course is what brings you closer to your islands of happiness and achievement and steers you away from the islands that don't offer either.

✓ *Look for ways to introduce more pleasure and more meaning into your life.*

✓ *Stop at good enough.* When the cost of an endeavor, decision, or activity outweighs the emotional benefit expected, you know you've spent too much time, energy, effort, and money in that space.

✓ *Surround yourself with happy people.*

4

Practicing Nonattachment

Most people put conditions on their happiness. They think, "I will be happy when I buy that mansion, when I get that promotion, when I drive home that Mascrati." Such thinking is a direct result of getting tangled up in the twisted logic of outside-in happiness, in which your emotional state is dependent on external circumstances. By now you should be able to see that this is a fool's game. If you become attached to the idea of something turning out a particular way — if that outcome becomes a prerequisite for your being happy — then you are giving away your power to control the way you feel. One of the most direct steps you can take toward being happy today, therefore, is to stop attaching conditions to happiness. You will feel better about yourself immediately if you detach your happiness from success, accomplishment, and material possessions, if you divorce who you are from what you have, what you do, what you've accomplished, and who your friends are.

Detaching doesn't mean you stop wanting to be successful. Practicing the art or philosophy of nonattachment doesn't mean you stop wanting, for that matter. That won't work. It's not possible to squelch desire. Just detach. Detach from the need to be successful in order to be happy. No, go further. Detach from the need for anything or anybody to be different in order for you to be happy right here and right now.

Emotions Are the Ultimate Currency

When you attach no conditions to your happiness, you are saying, in effect, that nothing matters more than how you feel now, right at this moment. "How it feels" becomes your barometer or measuring stick instead of "how it looks," "how it sounds," or "how it seems." You begin to judge your life not in terms of titles, promotions, brand names, and square footage, but in terms of the amount of joy and happiness that you feel on a daily basis.

Most of us are used to judging everything in terms of money, status, respect, fame, and possessions. These things or their symbols become like currency: we use them to assign comparable values to people, things, decisions, outcomes, and our progress in life. If you want to be happy, however, this is not the way to run your life. That's because emotions are the ultimate currency and anything else is counterfeit.

Our minds are not designed like computers. They are not designed to give us a neat printout of the rational arguments for and against a decision in life based on all the previous times we've faced a similar situation. The mind is more elegant and complex than this. The mind weighs the emotional bottom line from previous experiences and delivers the answer to us in a hunch, a gut feeling.

Emotions are important because if we did not have them nothing else would matter. If we had no emotions, we would have no reason for living or, ironically, for committing suicide. Emotions are the essence of life. They are the stickiest glue that bonds us to others and the sharpest sword that tears us apart. Emotions allow us to make meaning of everything. The point of doing, having, or being anything is to feel better. Making people objectively better off does nothing for them unless it also makes them subjectively better off.

Emotion is the ultimate currency, not money, success, fame, respect, status, or anything else. Emotion is the ultimate currency because all of these other forms of currency are valued only to the extent that they are supposed to make you feel better, to allegedly buy you more of one thing — happiness. By making joy your measuring stick, by redefining success in terms of the amount of happiness you feel, you can make emotion your ultimate currency and become happier today.

Expectations

Expectation is the source of all misery in the world. In order to be happy, therefore, you must give up your expectations; you must detach from the need for having specific outcomes or specific results. You must not expect anybody to do or not do anything in particular and you must not expect anything in particular to happen or not happen. This is the law of expectation. When you learn to accept and love what is, you open yourself up to a world of possibilities. You must learn to let the present be what it is — a gift in its own right — without wrapping it and coloring it with expectations of what it might become, good or bad.

One of the most legendary and most successful basketball coaches of all time, Phil Jackson, expressed this principle well: "In basketball — as in life — true joy comes from being fully present in each and every moment, not just when things are going your way. Of course, it's no accident that things are more likely to go your way when you stop worrying about whether you're going to win or lose and focus your full attention on what's happening right at this moment." Sometimes, in the pursuit of happiness, people forget that it's the happy moments — when strung together with meaning and purpose — that make for a happy life.

You can tell that you've violated the law of expectation when you feel negative emotion. The moment you feel disappointed, angry, frustrated, or resentful is the moment you've traded unconditional happiness for conditional happiness. You feel negative emotion only because you're comparing what is to what you think should be or could be. Every time you make that kind of comparison, you're jeopardizing your present moment. And as you jeopardize your present moment, you jeopardize your future moments, too, because unhappiness now leads to greater unhappiness later.

The moment you need somebody to think, speak, or act in a certain way to make you happy is the moment you surrender your happiness to circumstances outside of your control and render yourself powerless in the pursuit of happiness. The moment you need things to be different in order for you to feel different, you become the puppet and circumstances, people, and events outside of you become your puppet master, your Geppetto. This doesn't mean that you stop hoping for or wanting things to be different or better; it means that you stop *depending* on things being different or better in order to be happy right here and now.

The Law of Choices

The law of expectation is built on the law of choices, which states that everyone has the right to choose what he or she thinks, says, and does. Likewise, you have the right to choose what you think, say, and do. Because you cannot walk in another person's shoes, think in her head, speak from her mouth, or live in her life, you only waste your time and hers when you try to insert yourself into her experience.

The law of choices also states that, at any point in time, you can control only your *response* to another person's behavior, not the behavior itself. You can respond in four main ways: you can try to change the behavior; you can live with it and like it; you can live with it and hate it; or you can leave.

Trying to change the other person or the other person's behavior directly is futile. It's futile because, no matter how hard you try, only the other person can make the decision to change his or her behavior. You can attempt to influence his or her behavior, but remember, as the saying goes, a person convinced against his or her will is of the same opinion still.

That doesn't mean that you become a doormat or that you surrender to another person's every whim and wish. Quite the contrary. Sometimes consequences need to be established and boundaries need to be drawn. An authentically happy person — one practicing the art of nonattachment and abiding by the laws of expectation and choices — may need to enforce consequences, but she doesn't do it with any sense of disappointment, frustration, anger, or resentment. She understands that her happiness is her own and that, without expectation, she's the master of the weather in her own emotional skies. As such, the consequences feel less like punishment and more like a natural law of cause and effect asserting itself.

My Attachments

Throughout my life, I've struggled with my attachments. I've struggled with identity issues, too — identities are just another type of attachment. In high school, I was "smart" and "a basketball player." But when the college scholarships for basketball didn't come, I found myself lost and depressed. I had no identity, or so I thought. Never once did I consider continuing playing basketball just for the love of it. Since I couldn't play at the highest collegiate level, I decided not to play at all.

After school, I joined a consulting company, as I mentioned earlier. I was a "consultant." Nobody knew what that meant or what I really did, including my parents, no matter how many times I tried to explain it to them. Still, I introduced myself by telling people what job I held and what my business card said. Soon thereafter, I began thinking of myself in terms of the car I drove, the brand name of the clothes I wore, and the woman I was dating. Inevitably, I lost that job, I couldn't afford those cars, the clothes faded and went out of style, and the women slipped out of my life.

Later, when I moved to Miami, I attached to an identity as a "party promoter." Then I was a "model" and "actor." Eventually, though, I got tired of the charades and rather empty facades. I got smart. I found a happier life. Now, when people ask me what I do, I give them a very different response. I say, "I've decided to make a career out of enjoying myself." That may not be the answer they're looking for but it's my truth; I'm speaking it and I'm living it, too. It always catches them off-guard. I think they appreciate the fresh perspective.

I have a close friend who took this approach a step further. She went online and ordered five hundred business cards, which she calls "life cards." The cards have her name and contact information on them and they read: "Liver and lover of life." She hands them out to people she meets and wants to stay in touch with.

Sometimes we attach to concepts, ideas, or beliefs. Throughout my life — being the ruminator that I am — I have attached to various belief systems. First there was Christianity. Then there was Buddhism. Then I read a lot on existentialism. Then I was Muslim. Then I was a law of attraction fan. I've also attached to different political causes. Sometimes it was democracy. Other times it was charity. I was pro-choice one year. Another year my platform was justice and honesty. I was a "victim." I was "unhappy." It never ended. The labels never quit. And they brought me great suffering and unhappiness.

Sometimes I've attached to objects even more strongly than to beliefs or identities. I remember buying furniture at about the age of twenty-four. I told myself that a particular piece would be the last entertainment center or coffee table or couch I would ever need. After I bought the coffee table, I was satisfied for a couple of years knowing that, despite all else, I had resolved that living room issue. Then I had to get just the right set of dishes. Then I needed to get just the perfect bed. Then I bought some drapes. A rug came in the mail. I was trapped in my lovely little nest. The things I owned slowly but surely came to own me.

Other times in my life, I've attached to specific outcomes: a relationship working out, a check arriving in the mail, my landlord being friendly, my car starting up in the morning, getting to work on time, my body responding in a specific way to my workouts or my diets, people liking me, people paying attention to me, my birthday being remembered, the sun coming out, or food showing up on time. Things never turned out quite the way I expected when I did that. I was always setting myself up for disappointment.

Eventually, I decided to stop being attached to particular outcomes and identities. This doesn't mean I stopped hoping or intending for the best. Nor did I stop wanting things or believing in things or having causes, either. I didn't even stop planning or preparing for things, events, or people. I just decided to stop attaching to results, to needing things to work out a certain way for me to be happy, content, and at peace. I found ways to enjoy what I had, where I was, and what was within my immediate control, particularly my own thoughts. I separated my identity from my happiness. I made happiness my top priority. I found ways to be happy no matter what, right here and right now.

Get High off Your Own Supply

In the drug business, there's an expression: "Don't get high off your own supply." The idea, basically, is that if you're selling illicit drugs, one of the worst things you can do is to become a user. (No, I've never sold drugs and have no intention of doing so. But I have seen lots of movies.) If you get high off your own supply, not only are you killing yourself, but you're also killing any hope of making a profit since you're smoking it, injecting it, or swallowing it up and becoming a junkie, too. There are values hidden in that expression, believe it or not: self-sufficiency, independence, and responsibility.

In the happiness business, this expression needs to be turned on its head. That's what I've done in recommending that you *do* "get high off your own supply." This means that you should appreciate what you have and who you are and refuse to be dependent on other people to supply you with what you need to be happy. The values here are also ones of self-sufficiency, independence, and responsibility. Nice twist, no? In short, the faster you learn how to get a natural high off your own happiness supply, the happier and better off you'll be. This kind of natural high doesn't run out or wear off. In addition, you become more conscious and aware, not less so. When you stop the rat racing, status chasing, and pleasure chasing, you tune in to and tap into your own happiness supply, a supply that's self-replenishing.

When you get happy first, then you're happy and that's the point of it all anyway. But a side benefit is that when you get happy, you get lucky. When you learn to want what you got, you get what you want. The universe gives you more of what you're grateful for. In other words, happy people become successful people. They are happy-go-lucky, indeed.

But becoming happy requires that you become self-sufficient, that you make your happiness depend on you and you only. If instead you make your happiness contingent on things outside of yourself, you render yourself powerless in the face of unhappiness.

Detach from what you have and what you do. Detach from what you want and where you've been. Just be. Happiness will ensue. I promise. Your cork will float, if you let it. Practice the art of nonattachment, the philosophy of detachment. If you learn to be happy no matter what, success and all its trappings will follow.

◡∴◡

INSIDE-OUT HAPPINESS HABITS

✓ *Don't limit your happiness by giving it conditions.*
✓ *Remember that when you feel negative emotion it's a sign that you're comparing what is to what you think should be or could be.* Be in the present moment without judgment or expectations and be happy.
✓ *Be the master of the weather in your own emotional skies.* Don't make your happiness dependent on other people's behavior.
✓ *Get high off your own supply.* Make happiness dependent on you and you only.

5

Focusing on the Positive

[We] imagine that thought can be kept secret, but it cannot; it rapidly crystallizes into habit and habit solidifies into circumstance.

— JAMES ALLEN

One of the most important keys to happiness can be reduced to one word: *focus*. What are you focusing on? What are you attending to? Common sense tells us that one aspect of feeling good about life is paying attention to — that is, focusing on — the good stuff in your life. You see, focus is power. And if you can learn to focus with more persistence on those things in your life that make you feel good, you'll become happier almost immediately. I guarantee it. Focus is just about training your mind for happiness, through practice, and learning how to pay attention.

Happiness Training with Your Happiness Coach

You can train yourself in the skills of being happy. Happiness is achieved by training the mind and spirit. Training the mind is a matter of growing and cultivating mental discipline. You don't need a better body, more money, greater success or fame, or the perfect mate. You have everything you need to be happier right here and right now: a powerful mind. All you need to do is train it.

Mental strength is achieved the same way as physical strength: through practice and perseverance. If you want to be a professional athlete, like Tiger Woods, you practice with a competent teacher for thousands of hours before the age of eighteen. Through this process, you radically alter your brain, increasing the number of connections between the relevant neurons. The practiced thoughts and practiced behaviors become easier to execute, and what would be a challenge to an untrained person becomes second nature for you.

In a similar way, you can rewire your brain to more consistently create positive emotions. The plasticity of the brain is real. What fires together wires together. Your thoughts literally can reconstruct the physical structure that is your brain. You create and recreate good feelings by learning to deliberately and consistently guide your thoughts. You can get happier by consistently reaching for better-feeling thoughts. Better-feeling thoughts lead to better-feeling feelings. And the more you practice this, the easier it becomes, because your brain is actually changing.

As I've said before, it's not things that make you feel happy or unhappy. It's not people who make you feel jealous or loving. It's not events or experiences that make you feel nostalgic or regretful. It's how you think about a thing, person, event, or experience that makes you feel the way you do — and that can be changed through practice and discipline.

You and only you are responsible for the way you feel. Your unhappiness is not the fault of your parents, your friends, your job, your lack of money, your bills, your accident, a death. Likewise, your happiness is not the result of any event or particular situation, such as your new job, your new car, your new relationship, the award you won, your promotion, or the attention you get from your friends. It's not the events, experiences, or people themselves that make you happy or sad. It's the way you think about those events, experiences, or people that determines whether or not you derive any happiness from them.

Being happy is the cornerstone of all that you are. Nothing is more important than that you feel good. And you have absolute and utter control over that because you can choose the thought that makes you worry or the thought that makes you happy. You have the choice in every moment.

The only questions are these: What are you paying attention to? Is what you're paying attention to making you feel good or bad? That's it. That's the whole be-all and end-all of happiness right there in a nutshell.

Desultory Distraction

Before you can give your attention to the right thoughts and feelings, you have to learn how to pay attention, period. We live in an age of attention deficits, where the rule is desultory distraction. The background to our lives is a white noise of sensationalistic TV shows, pompous pundits, eight-second sound bites, and the cult of celebrity. The need to direct attention and guide thought is more compelling than ever. You need time to stop, check in with yourself, and then proceed to be led by your inner compass.

I have a small Boston terrier puppy named Daschle. He's the cutest little guy in the world, but he's got a major attention deficit disorder. Or maybe it's an attention surplus. I don't know. All I know is that we can't walk down the street without his ears perking up at the slightest breeze, the tiniest insect seducing his little twelve-pound body down the street after it, or the slightest sound distracting him from completing some bodily function. It's insane! But he's learning. After some practice, he now only chases chameleons and lizards down the street instead of straws, napkins, and paper bags. For him, that's progress. To a large extent, we all have trouble focusing. But like Daschle, we can learn to tune out the distractions and be a little more deliberate about where we focus.

Happy People Are Selective Sifters

Every person, event, experience, and circumstance in life has positive and negative aspects. Everything has the potential to make you feel good or to make you feel bad. In a similar way, when you boil it down, there are really only two basic emotions: fear and love. Every other emotion is some combination or shade of these two emotions, and they fall into two categories: the fear-based negative emotions and the love-based positive emotions.

Negative emotion is always based on fear or lack. Lack is about insecurity of some sort. Any time you feel negative emotion, you are feeling fear as you notice the apparent lack of security, safety, soundness, stability, or wholeness. Fear is faith that things won't work out.

Likewise, positive emotion is always based on love or faith in abundance. Abundance is about opportunity of some sort. Any time you feel positive emotion, you feel love as you notice the apparent evidence of security, safety, soundness, stability, and wholeness.

Since all emotions are the descendants of thoughts, how you focus your mind determines whether you feel negative emotions or positive emotions. Doesn't it make sense that the more you pay attention to things that make you feel good and the less you pay attention to things that make you feel bad, the better you'll feel? As Fulton J. Sheen once remarked, "Each of us makes his own weather, determines the color of the skies in the emotional universe which he inhabits." We use the brush of attentive focus to paint those emotional skies with colors from the palette of our thoughts.

When you are feeling negative emotion, it means that (1) you're paying attention to something important to you and (2) you're noticing the absence or potential absence of something you want to have or hold on to. Likewise, when you are feeling positive emotion, it means that (1) you're paying attention to something important to you and (2) you're feeling the presence of something you want, need, or value.

Happy people are selective sifters. They simply choose to pay attention to the aspects of situations, experiences, and people that help them feel the presence of what they want. No matter how negative an experience, situation, or individual seems, there is always some positive aspect to focus on. Unhappy people, ironically enough, are selective sifters as well, except that they latch onto the negative aspects of situations and people.

How you feel about any particular situation, then, depends on the direction of your focus. Are you focused on the negative aspects or the positive aspects? Are you focused on the lack of what you want or the presence of what you need? Is an unfulfilled desire discouraging or is it exciting?

Happiness is simple, if not easy. Happiness rests on your ability to find beauty wherever you look. If that ability doesn't come easy for you, then all you have to do is learn to direct your attention to the sunny side of the street, to the half-full glass, to the good news, and to things that make you feel good. Because attention works like a muscle, when you practice this habit regularly you get better and better at it as the positive-focus muscle becomes stronger and stronger.

There's a simple reason why happiness gets easier and easier with practice. You remember things better when you pay attention to them at the time they occur. So, the more positive things you pay attention to, the better job you will do in committing those positive things to memory. And when positive things fill your memory, it is easier to retrieve them. What that means is that even when you are in a bad mood, positive thoughts will be more accessible. If you are vigilant about keeping your focus on positive things, then, you will experience increasing levels of happiness. Happy thoughts and memories will flood your mind on their own, without your investing so much time and energy. Likewise, you can make unhappy feelings less common and less accessible by not paying attention to and not focusing on negative things as much when they occur. In time, you will forget them.

Starve the Bad Seed, Feed the Good One

When you give your attention to a thought or feeling, you feed it. This is true even when the attention is negative — when you reject a thought or feeling and try to put it out of your mind. If you're noticing it at all — in a good way or a bad way — you're giving it attention, feeding it, and allowing it to grow.

Research supports this. Findings suggest that any attempt to stop thinking a thought promotes preoccupation with that very thought. In one study, for instance, subjects were asked to try to stop thinking about a picture of a white bear that they had been shown earlier. This proved impossible for almost everyone. Such preoccupation with a forbidden thought was also observed when the thought had nothing to do with a specific image. When subjects were told they couldn't think about sex, for example, they failed. Apparently, trying to suppress a thought engages an automatic search capability in your brain that actively goes searching for the very thought that you are trying to escape. In fact, those who try the hardest to stop a thought succumb to it the most easily.

If you want to kill a thought or feeling, you have to starve it by withholding your attention. When a thought of anger, jealousy, fear, or worry creeps in, don't spend time fighting it — ignore it by distracting yourself with positive, absorbing, empowering thoughts and activities. Many people do this effectively with affirmations. The way to fight darkness is with light; the way to fight cold is with heat; the way to overcome evil is with good. You will never find any help in denials. Affirm the good, and the bad will stop showing up. Feed the good seeds and they'll keep growing. Starve the bad ones and they won't!

Your Emotional Guidance System

You may be thinking you have to "watch" every thought so you can separate the bad seeds from the good ones. Well, thankfully you don't. Inside of you there's a perfect instrument for sifting the bad seeds from the good seeds, and it runs on autopilot most of the time. Scientists say that we have about 60,000 thoughts a day. Paying full attention to all these thoughts every day would be impossible, so the job is taken over much of the time by what I call your emotional compass or guidance system. It makes you feel bad when bad-feeling thoughts are taking over, and good when positive thoughts prevail.

So, you simply have to learn to pay more attention to the emotional messages being sent to you by your emotional guidance system. By learning to be more sensitive to the way you feel about things, you will become more cognizant of the bad-feeling thoughts in your head. When you find your happiness dipping, realize that your emotional guidance system is telling you something, and then pivot or turn your attention to a different, positive aspect within that subject, or to a different, more positive subject altogether. It's that simple.

Most self-help experts or even traditional psychologists (as opposed to positive psychologists) will tell you to think more about your problems. I disagree. Doing so will only remind and convince you of all the reasons you're justified in feeling unhappy. This is the problem with most addiction centers or weight-loss clinics, too. When the focus and attention are on the problem, you only invite more of it.

Postpone problem solving until you're in a better mood. Focusing on what makes you feel bad will never make you feel good. Excessive thinking about your problems, the past, or why you aren't happy or successful will only work to convince you that you have good reasons to be unhappy. Once your cork starts floating again and you're in a better mood, your creativity, initiative, and problem-solving ability will return in spades and you'll find yourself making progress where you only spun your wheels before.

Think of your problems less, but don't think less of your problems. In other words, don't trivialize your problems, but *do* distract yourself from them by finding other engrossing things or activities to absorb your attention. Usually, physical activities or particularly challenging activities that require concentration are the best.

For me, running and weightlifting work well to put me in a positive mood. Cleaning is also very therapeutic for me. It works wonders when I'm feeling anxious, worried, and fearful. Somehow, bringing order to my outer world by cleaning out a closet, organizing the items in my apartment, rearranging furniture, or taking care of things always brings greater clarity and order to my inner world, too. Creating to-do lists and checklists does the same.

Some people like to meditate or practice yoga. These are both great activities that prevent you from giving your attention to negative thoughts. Different things work for different people. Through trial and error, find what works for you.

The Power of Shifting Attention

What we're really talking about here is learning to switch topics, change the station, or replace the scenery, in one form or another. In other words, becoming happier is about shifting your focus to the positive. If you can distract yourself from the bad-feeling experience long enough, your emotional cork will float again. And your life will change accordingly.

Positive focus is so easy that a five-year-old can do it. A landmark study conducted by Walter Mischel tested children's ability to delay immediate gratification. He gave kids the opportunity to eat one marshmallow now (immediate gratification condition) or wait for an unspecified period of time and then get to eat two marshmallows (delayed gratification condition). The children who were most successful in delaying gratification understood how to shift their attention by looking away from the temptation or by thinking about other enjoyable activities. They learned how to focus on something else. In essence, they understood the nature of successful distraction techniques. They intuitively knew that proper and effective distraction meant not just looking away from the temptation (the marshmallow) but also, and more importantly, looking for, and getting absorbed by, other enjoyable activities (the wall, the toys in the corner, etc.).

Incidentally, the study, conducted over the course of many years, also found that the ability to delay gratification through distraction was directly correlated with positive outcomes later in life. The number of seconds kids could wait to ring the bell for two marshmallows instead of one marshmallow predicted not only how positively parents viewed the kids later as teenagers but also the likelihood that the kids were admitted to a top university fifteen years later.

So, take a lesson from Mischel's five-year-olds. Learn the power of shifting your attention to something positive. If you're in a great relationship but get annoyed by certain things the person does, focus on what you love about the person. If you're in a good job but hate your boss, focus on those things at work that feel better. If you're going for a run and your legs hurt, give more attention to your arms. If you weigh more than you'd like to, focus on how healthy your body is and how much healthier you'd like it to be. I know it's hard at first, but everything is difficult until it's easy. Walking wasn't easy at first. English was a new language until it wasn't.

Feed the good stuff in your life with focus and attention and starve the bad stuff with indifference — when that's possible and not dangerous to your health, of course. It seems so elementary but it's amazing how few of us actually practice this consistently. And the more you practice this principle, the easier it will get. Pretty soon, you won't need to put so much effort into thinking about it. It will happen effortlessly and naturally. It will become second nature. With persistence, you'll be astonished at how powerful this practice of positive focus really can be.

~:~

INSIDE-OUT HAPPINESS HABITS

✓ *Focus on what feels good.* Practice. Then practice some more.

✓ *Learn to change the topic, station, or scenery when things aren't going well.*

✓ *Become more sensitive, not less, to the way you feel about things.* When you notice your happiness dipping, take a closer look at the thoughts behind those feelings.

✓ *Feed the good seeds in your life with attention and starve the bad seeds with indifference.*

✓ *Practice nonresistance.* What you fight, you invite. So don't try to stop a thought. Just observe it and question it. Or replace it with a more empowering one.

✓ *Don't try to solve problems when you're feeling bad.* Wait until you're feeling better.

6

Appreciating Yourself

The root of much unhappiness is comparison. Comparison gets in the way of healthy self-appreciation — and thus happiness — more than anything else. Because of comparison, hardly anybody is ever happy with what they get and nothing's ever good enough for practically everybody. That's because we measure our success in anything by comparing it to what others have or to what we have had before. In other words, whether you are happy with what you get depends on how it measures up to some norm. That norm depends on two things: what other people get (social comparison), and what you yourself are used to getting (habituation). It is hard for success in any form (money, status, prestige, and so on) to improve your happiness because as actual success rises, the norm by which success is judged rises in step.

A study, for instance, found Olympic bronze medalists to be happier than silver medalists. The bronze medalists, it turns out, tended to compare themselves with all the people who competed but won no medal at all, while the silver medalists compared themselves with the gold medal winners and tortured themselves with the belief that they could have — *should* have — won the gold. Similarly, in families, it has been found that the more your spouse earns, the less satisfied you are with your own job.

Because we constantly compare ourselves to others, we don't feel good about what we have and who we are. The grass seems perennially greener in your neighbor's lawn. Continuing with this metaphor, it might be said that the grass always seems to be greener in your neighbor's yard because (1) you're urinating on your own lawn and (2) you're looking at your neighbor's lawn from your lawn, and everything looks better from a distance. There is only one solution to this "grass is greener" problem: practicing self-appreciation. Self-appreciation involves both staying off of other people's lawns and taking care of your own.

Appreciate Your Own Lawn

A key ingredient in happiness is appreciating your life as it is. You can do this by keeping an appreciation log. Just list the positive aspects of things in your life. List the positive aspects of what you have and what you appreciate about your life and the people in it. And be sure to make a list of what you appreciate about yourself. Do this at least once a week — every day is even better. Science has found that the benefits of being grateful are optimized when you focus on appreciation at least once a week. This exercise isn't about wearing rose-colored glasses as much as it is about appreciating what's worthy of appreciation. Some things are just bad. If you can't change them, learn to accept them.

When you're feeling particularly frustrated, jealous, or hopeless, see if you can't sit down and write out a list of things you appreciate about your current situation. By doing so, you'll come to the realization that you have enough and do enough already. And when you do decide to get or do more, it will come from a positive, healthy, loving, inspired place instead of a dark, negative, and unhealthy bottomless pit.

To fully appreciate yourself and your life, you have to ignore what others think of you, what others have, and what others do. Only your thoughts influence your happiness. Others' thoughts of you do not affect your happiness. Only your thoughts about their thoughts affect how you feel. Only your thoughts about what they have and what they do influence your feelings of well-being. You can change your thoughts and you can't change theirs. What others think, say, do, or have has nothing to do with you.

The only opinion in the entire universe that is of importance to you is your own. And your opinion affects your entire life. Nobody else needs to get what you're doing or agree with it. So replace your shopping sprees, working sprees, pleasure sprees, complaining sprees, and unhappiness sprees with an appreciation spree. Shop for things to appreciate about your life and yourself, not for things to purchase or improve. Never admire somebody else's fortune so much that you become dissatisfied with your own.

Take Care of Your Own Lawn

An important way to appreciate your life is to take care of what and who you have in your life. Take care of the things in your life by giving them routine maintenance and keeping them clean and polished. Wash your car; dust your desk; use your kitchen to cook great meals instead of going out. When you care for them, your possessions will only grow in value. Take care of the people in your life in similar ways, figuratively speaking. Give your friendships routine maintenance. Check in on the people you care for; tell them you appreciate them. They'll appreciate you back.

My mother and father believed in taking care of things. They worked hard to provide us kids with some rather generous and expensive gifts and they hated seeing those gifts lost, broken, or going unused. Despite their admonishments, however, we would inevitably tire of that new bicycle, video game system, compact disc, or toy and toss it downstairs into the cellar or garage, never to be seen again. We'd do that every year with something or other. Somehow, though, my parents' lessons about taking care of things stuck with me. Just as frequently as we'd toss a random toy or gift into the cellar, we'd find one there, too. It was like Christmas in July. There was always at least one old Christmas or birthday gift sitting there just waiting for us to retrieve it. We'd pull that old baseball mitt, chipped wooden baseball bat, crippled doll, rusty bicycle, or deflated football from the crack or corner in which it slept and run upstairs as happy as you'd be after finding a long-lost friend. Then we'd break out the oil, the cleaning solutions, the wood glue, a rag or old T-shirt. And we'd go to work on that mitt, bat, doll, bike, or ball. Before too long, it looked and felt brand new. When we were done fixing it, we'd play with it as though we had just bought it from the store. Each and every time, I remember, I felt a mix of excitement and slight sadness that I had somehow unappreciatively let this great gift get musty, dusty, and old when it had treated me so well. From then on, whatever it was that I found I promised never to treat it so poorly again. For the most part, that's what I did. Every summer I seemed to learn the same lesson: what you appreciate and take care of only grows in value. That's the lesson here, too.

I'm still the same way. The only difference is that the toys are sometimes bigger and the stakes are sometimes higher. What's more, I believe in taking care of my relationships and myself the same way. For instance, I work out nearly every day. I get a haircut every Friday. Simple things. They make a difference in how I look, yes, but the important thing is that they make a difference in how I *feel*. People do notice that, and I notice it, too. I'm happier.

The Grass Isn't Greener Over There if You Don't See It

One reason it's so difficult to stop comparing yourself to others is that the media keep other people's imaginary lives constantly in your face. What's worse is that their lives are presented in ways that invite comparison, and that comparison always leaves you feeling worse about yourself. Nearly half of all the characters in prime-time social dramas are millionaires. And while two-thirds of real Americans work in blue-collar or service jobs, only 10 percent of television characters do. Advertising has similar effects, showing us worlds where people tend to live better than most of us do. According to one estimate, an extra hour a week watching TV causes you to spend an extra four dollars a week — on keeping up with the Joneses. So the more TV people watch, the more they overestimate the affluence of other people and the lower they rate their own relative income. The result is that they are less happy.

Viewing television may also reduce our happiness with our bodies and with our spouses, too. The psychologist Douglas Kenrick showed women a series of pictures of female models. He evaluated their moods before and after they looked at the pictures. After seeing the models, the women's moods darkened. After men saw the photos of the models, most felt less good about their wives. When you watch TV, everything real suffers by comparison.

That's the major reason I hardly ever watch television. If I said I watched television more than twenty times a year, I'd be exaggerating. That's surprising to most people, especially if they know that I used to be an actor and model. It's also surprising considering that some of my clients make a living through television. But it's true. As a kid, I learned how to play sports by watching sporting events on TV, found my role models in sitcoms, and even kept the TV on when I did my homework to keep me company.

I stopped watching so much television because, as I watched some of my favorite programs, I felt myself slipping ever so subtly into this little funk. I felt myself getting the slightest bit depressed. And I felt a little less worthy. After the show, I'd have a list of things that I now wanted, things that I hadn't even known I'd wanted. The strange thing is that before I watched each of those shows, I felt fine. I even felt happy. Afterward, though, I felt frustrated and disgusted with myself.

With the flick of a switch, not only do you see and hear how dangerous the world is and how we are headed for death and destruction, but you also get to see and hear how rich the rich are and how successful the successful are. This information makes what we all have worked so long and hard for look small, insignificant, and paltry in comparison. It all makes us ever more conscious and aware of what we lack relative to others.

To help myself stay off other people's lawns and appreciate my own, I started a media fast. You might try the same. Give it a shot and see how you feel. If you don't like it after a couple weeks, you can always go right back. The point isn't to stop finding ways to be entertained or to stop staying up-to-date with current events. The point is to be more sensitive to the way you feel when you're watching television or reading the news or watching videos online and to be more selective about what you do read, watch, or listen to.

I once read that the average American, by the time he or she is sixty years old, will have spent fifteen years staring at the TV screen. There's more to life than watching other people live it. And there's more to happiness than living vicariously through others.

It's amazing the difference that this media fast has made in my life. I'm much more in control of how I feel on a moment-to-moment basis, I have a much more optimistic perspective on the world, and I find myself surprisingly cheerful for no good reason at all. Try it and see if it works for you, too.

Perhaps it really is true: that what you see — and therefore seek — keeps you from the awareness of what you have. Limit the opportunities you have to peer at other people's grass, especially when it belongs to imaginary people and celebrities, and stay on your own lawn, where happiness truly does grow under your own two feet.

"I'm Good Enough, I'm Smart Enough, and Doggone It, I Like Me!"

Get happier by realizing and appreciating that you're good enough. Realize that who you are is a necessary step to becoming who you will be. Start appreciating what you have and who you are without asking for anything to be different. Keep lists of things you appreciate, share those lists, take care of what you have, and stop comparing yourself to anybody else in the world. Measure yourself by your best moments, not your worst. You're smart enough, you're good enough, and doggone it, people like you.

INSIDE-OUT HAPPINESS HABITS

✓ *Appreciate what you have and who you are, without asking for things to be different.* Keep a life appreciation log and a self-appreciation log. Learn to accept what you cannot change.

✓ *Stop comparing yourself to others.* Ignore what other people have and accomplish.

✓ *Try a media fast.* See how you feel after a week or two. If you feel better, continue it. If you don't, perhaps just be more selective about what you watch, read, and listen to.

7

Telling a Happier Story

The core lesson in this chapter is based on one you learned as a child: "If you don't have anything nice to say about somebody, don't say anything at all." We only have to modify this adage a little so that "somebody" includes yourself and the situations in which you find yourself. The idea is, very simply, to reach for a positive feeling before you speak, whether it's in your head or out loud. If you can learn to do this one thing, you'll be amazed at how much better you feel and, consequently, how much your relationships and your life will improve as well.

Start editing your speech by listening to what you think and say. Find ways to reframe, rework, or recraft unpleasant stories so that you find and share the upside — the appreciative side — of the story. For example, when you're on your way to a business meeting, don't repeat in your head the mistakes you made the last time; focus instead on appreciating this fantastic opportunity to be surrounded by other intelligent, competent individuals and how grateful you are to work for such a leading-edge company. When you're getting ready for a date, don't focus on how fat you look in your jeans, how badly your face has broken out, or how little money you have in your pocket. Instead, focus on how great it is that you have the opportunity to spend time getting to know somebody and how exciting it is that somebody's interested enough in you to devote an entire evening to you. When you're relating your day to your friend or partner, tell him or her what you found most intriguing, interesting, exciting, or delicious about your day. What was your favorite part of the day? What did you like most about your week? Who brought you the most joy? What inspired you the most? What are you most anticipating the following day, week, month, or year?

Always ask yourself: Is what I am about to say going to advance the cause of my vision, mission, and goals? Will it uplift the hearer? Will it inspire, motivate, and create forward momentum? If you hear a negative story, simply don't repeat it. Decide that that story has gone on long enough and be vigilant about not thinking about it or retelling it. This practice will eventually begin to shape your thoughts. And as you model this behavior yourself, the example you set for others will be a teaching mechanism for them, too.

Tell a Better-Feeling Story

You cannot be unhappy without an unhappy story. Negative emotion itself is not unhappiness. Only negative emotion plus an unhappy story equals unhappiness. Likewise, you cannot be happy without a happy story. Positive emotion itself is not happiness. It needs a happy story to equal happiness. Stories provide the value judgments and meaning that are needed for emotions to become a condition of happiness or unhappiness.

A friend provided a great example of this idea:

> My father died suddenly when I was working at a job that made me quite miserable. I went home for the funeral, and during the course of a painful week, I realized that my sorrow at my father's death was hard, but it wasn't toxic. We shared good memories, I found love with my siblings, I felt bad for my mother but also proud of the life they had shared for forty-five years. I learned that sorrow doesn't have to be toxic or ugly; it can be beautiful. And I realized that what was toxic and ugly was my job, so I went back and quit because I couldn't allow myself to remain in a position that felt so wrong. Something that is hard or challenging isn't necessarily "bad."

Improve the content of the story you tell every day about your life, and your life will become that ever-improving story.

Sometimes I joke with my new clients. They'll ask me how I'm doing and I'll say something like "Today is my favorite day of the week." They'll respond with something like "Wednesday? Wednesday is the best day of your week? Why?" Then I'll quip, "Every day is better than the day before it in some respect. I've learned more or done more or am expecting more or have more to be grateful about. So, yes, today is the best day of the week. And the same will be true tomorrow, and the day after that, and so on."

In order to successfully tell that better-feeling story, you have to look for a positive, appreciative feeling inside you before you speak. Once you find this feeling, you can speak from this positive, appreciative place, and then you can keep trying to improve or enhance or exaggerate that feeling. You will feel better and better as a result. That's the point of the storytelling.

Language doesn't just describe our world; it creates it. Consider some findings. A recent study of young children found that the kids who heard the most words at home while they were growing up did the best scholastically and continued to do the best throughout grade school. Further, the kids who heard the most words also heard the most constructive words (words of encouragement, hope, empowerment, and love), and these kids excelled at bonding, exhibited the best behavior and self-esteem, and tended to view the world in the most positive terms. One lesson of the study is clear: it's through language that we create the world, because it's nothing until we describe it.

Debbie Downer

One of my favorite *Saturday Night Live* sketches used to be "Debbie Downer." Debbie Downer, a character played by

Rachel Dratch, persistently shared bad news about some new disease, world calamity, or local disaster. She made negative remarks at even the most uplifting social gatherings and in the most positive personal conversations. She brought down the mood of everyone around her. You might remember her telling downer stories like this one: "Did you guys hear about that train explosion in North Korea? The media is so sensitive there, so secretive. They may never know how many people perished." And here is another: "Wow, you guys. Disney World really is fun. It makes me feel like a kid again. I mean, the time before my two-year stint at Children's [Hospital]."

Don't be like Debbie Downer. In the sketch, her comments were funny because they contrasted so strongly with what was going on around her (and reminded us of people like her), but Debbie's way of telling stories makes for an unappealing, unflattering, unproductive, and disempowering way to live your life.

Speak more and more about what you want and less and less about what you don't want, and your life will begin to follow your words. Your feelings are your point of attraction, meaning that happy feelings lead to successful life outcomes and unhappy feelings lead to unsuccessful life outcomes. Scientific evidence supports this fully, if you'll remember. When you tell a better-feeling story, you improve how you feel and your feelings begin to shift in a new, positive, appreciative direction. As you tell the new story, you come to believe it; this positive belief creates positive feelings, and with positive feelings come positive outcomes.

Consider how this worked for actor and comedian Jim Carrey. One day, as a struggling Canadian comic and actor, he wrote himself a check for ten million dollars, postdated it "Thanksgiving 1995," added the notation "for acting services rendered," and carried it in his wallet from that day forth. After he made *Ace Ventura* in 1994, Carrey's asking price was twenty million dollars.

If you can't bring yourself to fantasize quite the way Jim Carrey did, you can always think of your situation the way I did when I began my coaching practice. Like Pierre S. DuPont IV, I'd repeat to myself over and over again: "I'm in a wonderful position: I'm unknown, I'm underrated, and there's nowhere to go but up." The important thing was that I was telling a better-feeling story based in truth.

Tell Your Highest Truth

Telling a better-feeling story doesn't mean sugarcoating reality or being dishonest. It's about telling the highest truth about yourself and your life. Telling the better-feeling story is about surveying all of the information at an emotional level and then choosing the best and the most positive, empowering, happiness-producing angle to spin. So telling the better-feeling story is less about fairy tales and fantasies and more about telling the best of what happened or telling the best of what may be coming. Telling the better-feeling story sounds like this: "What I liked about that was..." and "My favorite part about that was..."

Don't get caught up in trying to find the perfect words for your story. The exact words aren't important. What matters is how you feel when you think those thoughts, speak those words, or take that action. As Stanley Kubrick once said, "The truth of a thing is the feel of it, not the think of it."

If you're not telling something that you believe and is true for you, what you're really saying is that you feel that you're lying to yourself. That doesn't feel good. And feeling good is the point. To tell a better-feeling story based in truth, then, you have to look for a positive but honest feeling inside yourself before you speak. Then you can speak from this positive feeling and continually enhance it.

You have to find a credible and believable story based on facts. You rewrite the plot a little while being true to who you really are. You can't just paste smiley stickers on a broken relationship or paint happy faces on empty bank accounts. It's more than that. Authentic happiness is about the heart and the head. It's about emotion and reason, feelings and fact. It can't be a snow job. It's got to be believable and credible. And you make it believable and credible by finding evidence to support what you want to believe and by practicing telling the better-feeling story.

Sometimes, the bad-feeling stories we tell ourselves are very far from the truth and retelling them is just a matter of gaining perspective. One time, a friend and I were pulling out of his parking lot and a young woman approached us with the strangest expression on her face. My friend and I were both in good spirits so we thought she was laughing. She was actually terrified. When she approached us, she said nothing. Despite our persistent questions, she didn't respond. Then, finally, a light went on and we realized she was having a panic attack.

Apparently, she had lost her wallet and she couldn't find her friends or remember their phone numbers. She was a long way from home and was afraid her friends had left her. With time her anxiety passed and she got perspective. From there, I helped her to tell a better-feeling story based in fact. She had made a number of assumptions that were not only unprovable but also improbable. We rewrote those assumptions by questioning them. Instead of telling a story about her friends abandoning her and leaving her alone two thousand miles from home, she began telling a story about her friends being just as lost and confused as she was. As we looked for things to appreciate together — like the great weather, the chance meeting and new budding friendships, a reliable boyfriend who was willing to wire her money, and the opportunity for her to spend more time in a beautiful, sunny city with lots to do — her mood lifted and she felt much better.

Edit Your Life

Telling the better-feeling story is about retelling old, stale, disempowering, negative stories in new, fresh, positive, empowering, and better-feeling ways. And telling the better-feeling story means telling the best of what's happening or the best of what could happen. As you can imagine, this is an art. It is also a skill, and like any skill, it can be learned through practice.

But start where it's easy. The first step can be cutting worse-feeling stories out of your life. Begin with the stories other people tell: decide not to read, watch, listen to, talk about, or think about stories that make you feel bad. Then eliminate your own bad-feeling stories. Decide never to speak of yourself or your affairs in a discouraging or disparaging way. Decide never to admit the possibility of failure and never to speak in a way that infers failure as a possibility. Decide never to speak of the times being hard or the business conditions being doubtful.

To keep this simple, ask yourself, "Does this story make me feel better or worse?" If it makes you feel worse, stop telling it or refuse to listen to it. Also ask yourself, "Am I using language that empowers me or disempowers me? If the words disempower you, stop using them.

Here are a few examples of expressions that might be eliminated:

- *Should* and *shouldn't* and *have to*. Who says you should or should not? When you understand the concept of separate realities, what you should and shouldn't do or say becomes irrelevant.
- *Need to*. In the broadest sense, you don't need to do anything except live and then die. Let go of your scarcity- and need-based feelings of fear and step back into your freedom. Realize that you choose everything you do because you want to do it for one reason or another. There may be consequences if you don't do something but that doesn't mean that you should or need to do it.
- *But*. You split your focus and dilute your power every time you use this word because it leads you toward cognitive dissonance and conflicting thoughts.
- *Don't forget*. Thinking in terms of what you don't want to happen doesn't work. Think about it. If

someone says "don't look," you immediately look. Rephrase by saying "remember" to do something.

- *I can't.* How do you know you can't do something? Have you tried? Just because you haven't done it before doesn't mean you can't do it.
- *You can't.* How do you know he or she can't? What makes you the judge?

Changing Your Stories

After you've eliminated the bad-feeling words and stories, the next step is to replace them with better-feeling ones. For example, you can replace *should* and *shouldn't* with *I can choose, if I really want, to. . . .* Similarly, you can replace *don't forget* with an affirmation such as *I remember to. . . .* Here are more examples of how you can transform a disempowering story into a better-feeling, empowering story:

	WHAT YOU MIGHT NORMALLY SAY OR THINK	THE BETTER-FEELING STORY
MONEY	"I'm always broke."	"I'm prosperous in ways that can't be measured with money."
	"Money doesn't grow on trees or just fall out of the sky."	"I always somehow have more than enough to survive. I live in comfort and security."
	"The economy is a wreck and there are no jobs."	"There are always people who prosper in a bad economic climate and I'm one of them."

	WHAT YOU MIGHT NORMALLY SAY OR THINK	THE BETTER-FEELING STORY
CAREER AND PROFESSIONAL LIFE	"My job sucks."	"My favorite part of my work is . . ."
	"My boss is an a#$%!."	"My boss has taught me a great deal about what kind of person I want to be and what I stand for."
	"I don't know what I want to do and I'm never going to figure this out."	"Every experience helps me to get clearer and clearer about what I want and who I am. I've made so much progress and I'm appreciating this process of elimination."
RELATIONSHIPS AND SOCIAL LIFE	"I'm going to be alone forever."	"I'm appreciating the freedom and flexibility that I now have and I look forward to sharing that with whomever I rendezvous with each day."
	"There are no good women (or men) left. They are all taken."	"There are six billion people on this planet and many, many of them are unattached like me. I meet people every day who are fun, appreciate me, and add lots of pleasure and meaning to my life."
	"I'm never going to get married and have kids because I'm getting old."	"I'm learning more and more to appreciate what I have and I'm eagerly but patiently anticipating the company of other people in my life."

	WHAT YOU MIGHT NORMALLY SAY OR THINK	THE BETTER-FEELING STORY
RELATIONSHIPS AND SOCIAL LIFE (CONTINUED)	"You always do that."	"I'm getting better and better at finding your positive aspects. It's not your responsibility to make me feel good; it's mine. And you're helping me get really good at recognizing this."
	"All men are dogs. All women are liars."	"I appreciate honest people and I find them whenever I actively look for them. All men and women are just trying to find their way, trying to be happy. As I'm less judgmental of them, I'll learn to be less judgmental of myself, too."
HEALTH AND BODY	"I'm fat."	"I'm anticipating the unveiling of the slimmer, healthier body that lives within me."
	"I hate my body."	"My favorite part of my body is . . ."
	"I'm always getting sick and my immune system sucks."	"I'm feeling healthier every day and I'm taking action to get healthier every day and that makes me feel better."

Jessica's Better-Feeling Story

One of my most rewarding clients was a woman I'll call Jessica — a single mother who had suffered through a series of physically and verbally abusive relationships and felt that she couldn't attract or meet a "good man." First I asked her to make feeling good her top priority. I explained to her that while she was not and never would be responsible for her boyfriends' behavior, her decision to endure those past experiences stemmed in part from a lack of self-esteem. If at a deep level she didn't feel that she deserved abusive treatment, she wouldn't have invited those experiences, put up with them, or stuck around to play them out. I also helped her to understand that all of it would turn around the moment she started treating herself better and started holding herself in higher regard. In a way, she needed to be that person she wanted to attract, and she needed to treat herself the way she wanted others to treat her.

Then, we rewrote her history and the story she was telling about her two failed marriages. I stressed the importance of telling the positive story that made her feel good (based on facts, of course) and not telling it "the way it is." She did this by looking for and listing the lessons that those relationships had taught her (such as the importance of self-love, how resilient and strong she actually was, how you get what you focus on).

Next, I asked her to start taking a more appreciative approach to everything she had in her life. She found that her appreciative approach changed her focus and, therefore, the experiences she had. She got more of what she focused on. Perhaps not surprisingly, this inside-out, appreciation-flavored approach in turn activated a similar shift in others. Then their more optimistic, appreciative attitude and behavior only made Jessica's now rose-colored life that much rosier.

But — and this is key — Jessica focused on herself and her own life; she didn't make other people or their lives her business. In so doing, she created an exponentially happier life from the inside out.

Eventually Jessica's new approach led to less effort and more reward because it used what was already working and allowed her to eliminate what was not working. She came to realize, she said, that "God gives you more of what you're grateful for." What she couldn't appreciate, I urged her to overlook. She did this by distracting herself with other things that she did appreciate and love. Finally, she agreed to repeat a few daily affirmations. The affirmations I created were specifically tailored to her issues and her problems.

With practice, persistence and patience, Jessica rewrote the stories of her past relationships in ways that were inspiring, uplifting, and empowering but still truthful. By focusing on the lessons she learned from those men, affirming those lessons every day, and looking for (and listing) things to appreciate within every man she met, Jessica very quickly found herself in the most loving and compassionate relationship of her life.

AFFIRMATIONS

Repeating affirmations is a way of bringing better-feeling, empowering stories into your life right away by finding and affirming the good that exists in your life already. Here are some affirmations I've suggested for clients. Try them for yourself. At first, you may feel silly saying them but, with practice, they'll take root and may make a big difference in your life.

- I've made my happiness dependent on me and me only.
- Because I cannot control conditions, I control myself beautifully, effortlessly, and successfully, thought by thought.
- I'm free of all addictions to people and things. I'm addicted only to feeling good and the only person who can (or ever has) made me feel good (or bad) is me. I love myself and I love my independence and I'm living that every moment of my life.
- I am realizing more and more that I am — and have always been — self-sufficient and independent.
- I'm a strong, loving, independent, freedom-seeking woman (or man). I love myself and that love is independent of what anybody else says or thinks.
- I'm becoming more and more confident and comfortable in my own skin.
- My thoughts and opinions are louder and clearer than the thoughts of everyone else out there and

that means I'm mastering my life, one thought at a time! I unconditionally love myself inside and out and nothing can change that.

- I'm God's gift to myself. God is perfect and, because I'm God's creation, I'm perfect as I am.
- Everything I've ever needed or wanted, I was born with. The vortex of well-being that I call "boyfriend" or "girlfriend" or "mother" or "friend" or "job" or "relationship" is really me and the thoughts that I choose.
- I've made myself my top priority. I've made feeling good my dominant intent.

Act as If

When in doubt, follow Dale Carnegie's advice: "Act as if you were already happy, and that will tend to make you happy." In other words, conduct yourself the way a happy person would. Take on a happy person's mannerisms, characteristics, and habits. Tell the stories a happy person would tell. Then watch yourself get happier.

Learn to be your own best advocate. Be more careful and deliberate about what you think and say. Reach for a positive feeling before you speak. Tell better-feeling stories and you'll experience better-feeling feelings — you will become happier from the inside out. And because happiness leads to success, your life will follow your words.

.:~

INSIDE-OUT HAPPINESS HABITS

✓ *Choose your language carefully.* Edit your speech according to how it makes you feel.

✓ *Reach for a positive feeling before you speak.*

✓ *Start telling a better-feeling story based in fact.* Notice the language you use. Notice the content of your discussions. Notice the tone of your telephone conversations. Pay attention to the themes of your text messages.

✓ *Make your vocabulary more positive.* Learn and reach for optimistic words and optimistic language. If you use terms that describe positive, healthy emotional states and feelings, you'll be surprised how your actual emotional state changes accordingly.

8

Embracing Adversity

Sunshine is delicious, rain is refreshing, wind braces us up, snow is exhilarating; there is really no such thing as bad weather, only different kinds of good weather.

— JOHN RUSKIN

In Miami Beach, we have our fair share of hurricanes and hurricane warnings. Because most of the city is built just above sea level, we also get our fair share of floods. What I've always found so incredible about the people here is that they seem to weather storms so well. When a hurricane is on its way, they don't panic. If they don't already have hurricane supplies, they go purchase all the necessary materials and close their hurricane shutters. Then they figure out where the hottest party is going to be for that night — and the one after, and the one after that! And if they aren't into partying, they call their closest friends and go to a movie, rent a movie, or make a movie, depending on the kinds of friends they have. Residents don't run for the hills, book the first flight out of Dodge, or break down in a fit of tears. They are more resilient than that. They know that the storm will pass.

Often the storm ends up being not as bad as predicted. On the few rare occasions when the storm is worse than expected, people still remain calm. If an evacuation is ordered, people seem almost enthusiastic to drive off to a nearby shelter. There's no rush, no fear, and very little confusion or chaos. It's quite a sight. The tourists, of course, are different. They are filled with sheer terror. What they don't know is that bad weather always looks worse through a window.

Miami residents, for the most part, are used to the fire drills that are part and parcel of living in a tropical climate. They know that dark clouds can appear out of nowhere and deliver a torrential downpour. They also know that after a two-hour rainfall the skies can open up and it can turn into the most wonderful, brilliantly sunlit day you could ever imagine.

The weather in Miami — alternately stormy and calm — is a lot like our lives. Sometimes storms wreak havoc and things don't work out as we had hoped. That's a given. It's how we cope with, respond to, and rebound from the adversity in life that makes all the difference. Happy people handle adversity much as the residents of Miami handle storms and hurricanes: they take it in stride and appreciate how it can shake things up for the better. When you practice happiness from the inside out, adversity reveals hidden strengths, weeds out some relationships and cultivates those that remain, and clarifies what's most important in your life.

Hidden Strengths and *The Wizard of Oz*

You are never stronger, more focused, and more clear about what you want than when you are experiencing extreme adversity. You've heard of women lifting cars several feet into the air to save their babies' lives? Well, there you go. But the kind of strength I'm referring to isn't just the physical kind. It's also the psychological and emotional kind.

The film *The Wizard of Oz* (1939) illustrates well how adversity can uncover hidden strengths by forcing us to rise to the occasion. In case you don't remember, Dorothy Gale lives a simple life in Kansas with her Aunt Em, Uncle Henry, and three colorful farm hands. One day Miss Gulch, a neighbor, is bitten by Dorothy's dog, Toto. Miss Gulch takes Toto away, by order of the sheriff, over the protests of Aunt Em and Uncle Henry. Toto escapes and returns to Dorothy, who is momentarily elated. But Dorothy soon realizes that Miss Gulch will return. She decides to take Toto and run away in search of a better life "somewhere over the rainbow." On their journey Dorothy encounters a fortune-teller who, out of concern for Dorothy, tricks her into believing Aunt Em is ill. Dorothy rushes back to the farm but is then carried away with the house and without her family by a sudden tornado.

When Dorothy awakens, she discovers that she has unwittingly killed the Wicked Witch of the East. Glinda, the Good Witch, magically slips the dead witch's ruby slippers onto Dorothy's feet and instructs her to visit the Wizard of Oz if she is intent on returning home.

During her journey along the yellow brick road, Dorothy meets several companions who all want a better, happier life, and they think the Wizard can deliver it to them. The Lion desires courage, the ability to face fear. The Tin Man wants a heart, the ability to feel compassion. The Scarecrow desires a brain, the virtue of wisdom.

Dorothy is in search of a better life herself. In addition, the opening scenes of the movie showed Dorothy to be lacking in each of the virtues that her new companions want to acquire. One of the farmhands accused her of not using her brain (lack of wisdom); she ran away when things got difficult (lack of courage); and she left her family (lack of compassion).

By the end of the movie, however, things have changed quite significantly for Dorothy. The adversity Dorothy encounters reveals in her a number of hidden strengths. She expresses courage when confronting the Wicked Witch of the West and when approaching the Wizard; she shows care, kindness, love, and compassion for her new friends by consistently encouraging them to march forward in search of their dreams. Likewise, she shows the same kind of compassion and love when she decides to return to Kansas. In fact, that decision is probably the greatest testament to her transcendent experience and her character development because she comes to the realization that "if you can't find your heart's desire in your own backyard, then you never really lost it to begin with." She stops looking for happiness in other places and begins to truly understand that everything she needs to live a happy life is inside her.

The message is clear. All of us have what we need already; all that we desire we have already. From this perspective, happiness is less about improving things or getting things than it is about appreciating things, accepting ourselves, cultivating things, and expressing pre-existing strengths. The question becomes: "Which part of myself do I want to show up in this present time-space reality?"

Life's trials and tribulations provide the opportunities for character expression. In this vein, there is no such thing as finding yourself; there is only expressing different parts of yourself when adversity presents its challenges. In *The Wizard of Oz*, adversity is clearly a catalyst for character strength and virtue development. And all of the characters own and exhibit their virtues long before the Wizard awards them the physical symbols of those virtues.

Applying the Lessons

As you plan for future endeavors of all sorts, I hope that you can apply some of the simple yet age-old lessons of *The Wizard of Oz*. First and foremost, I would like you to remember the core message of chapter 6 on self-appreciation: You are whole as you exist now in the time-space continuum. Second, it's your choice whether to exercise any particular strength. While certain strengths seem always to be available and their expression comes naturally, others may be hidden and you will never know they are there until you decide to respond to adversity.

As you look forward, you should be encouraged by the role that adversity will play in your life. While you will work, of course, to minimize hardship and manage risk as much as possible, you should be comforted by the possibility that adversity, when it does happen, will facilitate growth and help in the cultivation, or expression, of character strengths and virtues. People need adversity, setbacks, and sometimes even trauma to reach their highest levels of strength, fulfillment, and personal development. In fact, people often become happy and successful because of adversity, not in spite of it. Rising to a challenge often helps one uncover hidden skills and talents, and this kind of revelation changes one's self-concept forever.

Indeed, resilience and equanimity in the face of adversity is perhaps the most crucial ingredient to living a happy, healthy life. More than anything else, it's what determines how high we rise above what threatens to wear us down, from illness to relationship challenges and economic crisis. Everyone needs resilience. Furthermore, resilience, like optimism, is not just an ability that you're born with or not but a skill that anyone can learn and improve on. You can boost resilience by changing the way you think about adversity.

The same attitudes that help you face adversity and allow it to draw out your strengths can also help you come to terms with the past. Many people view the past with regret because they look back and see mistakes and failures. This has the same negative consequences as viewing upcoming challenges with anxiety and fear. You must realize that there's no such thing as failure; there's only feedback. The mistakes you've made in the past have provided you with opportunities to get clearer and clearer about who you are and what you are to be. Every experience of your life, therefore, has been a blessing — nothing more, nothing less. If you condemn your past experiences, you condemn yourself — and this means you disempower yourself and miss out on happiness.

Other Advantages of Adversity

Adversity doesn't just reveal hidden strengths. It also helps weed out fair-weather friends, and it strengthens the friendships that remain. In a storm, the people you call — or call on — are usually your closest and best friends. You may not have talked to them for years, but when times get tough, you always find out who is really there for you.

I have seen this advantage of adversity play out in Miami. Sometimes, I used to joke that Miami was a sunny place for shady people. It can be. Any place can be. When adversity strikes, relationships are affected. The strong ones get stronger and the weak ones disappear. When you cut the grass, the snakes will show.

Adversity also allows you to slow down, take stock, and reevaluate what is most important in your life. It brings things into sharper contrast, which helps you choose the right job, your best friends, and the happiest life path. Sometimes you have to experience who you *are not* in order to know who you really *are*. When you learn to make peace with where you are, you can make different, higher, more loving, more joyous, more evolved choices about who you will become.

Variety Allows Preference;
Contrast Produces Desire

Life will never be perfect. It will never be perfect because you will always be facing some new challenge in your life. You can never get to a place where you are immune from difficulty or misfortune. If you live in a tropical paradise, storms can occur suddenly and without warning. If you live on the beautiful Great Plains, tornadoes can strike at any time. Some places experience more earthquakes, others have to cope with tsunamis, floods, or forest fires. In any case, life will never be devoid of the bad stuff.

In fact, life is beautiful because of the variety and contrast provided by adversity. It's the bad stuff, the adversity in life, that produces desire. Without adversity, there'd be no room for preference, no opportunity to make a higher choice. And preference allows desire to be born. Without contrast and, therefore, desire, life would be pleasureless and meaningless. Without the bad stuff in life, there'd be no great causes to support and no great pleasures to indulge in, either. Who would want to be happy all day every day forever? If someone told you that you couldn't ever be hungry or horny or thirsty again or have desire again, how would you feel? If you weren't sometimes deprived of what you want, how would you know what satisfaction felt like? There can be no wave without a trough. It's the sour that makes the sweet even sweeter.

You are never clearer about what you want than when you are experiencing what you do not want. Your desire is never stronger than when you find yourself in a bad way.

You're the hungriest when you've gone without food, the thirstiest when you've gone without drink, the most health conscious when you've been sick, and the horniest when you've gone without sex.

Now none of this is to say that war, natural disasters, disease, and destruction are good things. It's only to say that there are positive and negative aspects to every situation, place, and person. Whether you weather that adversity well or not is your response-ability — it depends on your *ability* to *respond*. Who will you choose to be in response to those moments? And what value will you extract from those experiences? It's that decision that separates the happy people from the unhappy.

Choose Happy over "Realistic" or "Right"

Adversity can cause you to color your expectations for the future in negative ways. Even if this seems like the realistic thing to do, it isn't good for your happiness. Some studies indicate that happy people tend to unrealistically exaggerate the likelihood of things turning out well, whereas unhappy people are much more realistic and accurate in their expectations of what the future holds. Interestingly enough, however, the realists don't benefit from being more accurate. That's right: if the realists are indeed wiser, it's to their ultimate detriment.

This is just another way of saying that optimism is a key ingredient for happiness. A great deal of scientific research shows this to be true. While realists and pessimists often find themselves powerless and at the mercy of their environment, optimists exercise jolliness in the face of defeat, failure, and loss and as a result remain happier. Both attitudes are really self-fulfilling prophecies. If you remain optimistic in the face of adversity, you are likely to continue to have reason for optimism in the future. If, on the other hand, you approach adversity with a more "realistic" attitude, chances are that future outcomes will confirm that you were right *not* to expect the best.

All great champions, most of whom are optimists, have become great because of — not in spite of — great adversity. Michael Jordan, a perennial optimist, once said, "I have missed more than nine thousand shots in my career. I have lost almost three hundred games. On twenty-six occasions I have been entrusted to take the game's winning shot . . . and missed. And I have failed over and over and over again in my life. And that is why . . . I succeed." If ever there was a case for optimism, this is it.

Being realistic doesn't come with any real rewards. Pessimists get depressed more easily, achieve less at work than their talents alone would predict, and suffer poorer physical health and weaker immune function. All in all, life for pessimists is not as pleasurable as it should be. In the long run, even if the pessimist is proved right, the optimist still has a better time on the trip. In other words, people who are realistic are only *temporarily* "right," because their lack of optimism can result in even worse outcomes than they expected.

Every person thinks he or she is right anyway. So the question isn't who's right or who's wrong. The question is: Who is most in alignment with herself and living most harmoniously with life? Who is bending most effortlessly with the natural course of life? Whose life is really going the best, most of the time?

In fact, because optimists, by definition, persevere in the face of their greatest tribulations, they're not only more likely to smile through it and experience less unhappiness but also more likely to turn it all around. For optimists, their greatest trial becomes their greatest triumph. And in most cases, as we saw earlier in the discussion in chapter 2 about happiness leading to success, optimists are successful across multiple life domains. Optimists, then, end up being right — in real life — just as often as, if not more often than, pessimists. Things do work out. Life is fair.

Even when pessimism is well founded, pessimists don't weather the adversity as well as optimists. The main difference between unhappy people (the majority of whom are pessimists) and happy people (the majority of whom are optimists) is how they choose to experience, or respond to, similar situations in their life. As Helen Keller recognized, "No pessimist ever discovered the secret of the stars, or sailed to an uncharted land, or opened a new doorway for the human spirit." Even if happy people don't know enough to be prudent, they are the ones who attempt the seemingly impossible and achieve it, generation after generation.

If you truly want to be happy, then, choose happiness over "being right" or being realistic at every turn, at every opportunity. And follow all the other habits of optimistic people: Look for reasons to feel good. Find things to appreciate. See beauty everywhere you look. Sift through the experiences of your daily life and commit to finding the positive aspects of whatever it is you are looking at. The behaviors and attitudes of optimism are the best allies you'll have in weathering difficult times and challenges, and they'll help open your eyes to all the benefits of adversity. There are people who prosper in the worst of times, and there are people who struggle even in the best of times. Whether you prosper or struggle is largely a matter not of the circumstances that surround you but of the conditions that exist within you.

Learned Optimism

If by temperament you don't naturally lean toward an optimistic view of life, don't worry — you can learn to be more of an optimist. Optimism, from a scientific perspective, is more than just turning your gaze to the sunny side of the street or calling the glass half full. Optimism is a way of explaining the causes of good events and bad events that empowers you and supports your happiness. This way of explaining what life serves you up doesn't come naturally for everyone, but there is absolutely nothing preventing you from learning how to do it.

Let's take a closer look at this way of thinking about optimism. Optimists explain good events in personal, pervasive, and permanent ways, and they explain bad events in impersonal, temporary, and local ways. Pessimists tend to do exactly the opposite: when something good happens, it's just a fluke, and when something bad happens, it's a manifestation of the way things are. An optimistic child, for example, might explain a bad event, such as getting a bad grade on an exam, by saying, "the test was hard (impersonal), the course is getting easier (temporary), and I'm really better at a lot of other subjects (local)." A pessimistic child, in contrast, might explain the same event by saying, "I'm really dumb (personal), I'm always going to be dumb (permanent), and I'm dumb in every subject (pervasive)."

So, learning to be an optimist is simply a matter of learning to explain good events in personal ("me"), pervasive ("all situations"), and permanent ("all times") ways and bad events in impersonal ("not me"), local ("not all situations"), and temporary ("not all times") ways. If you want to learn more about teaching yourself how to be optimistic, consider reading *Learned Optimism* by Martin Seligman or *The Resilience Factor* by Karen Reivich.

Freedom of Action and Freedom of Thought

Without variety or contrast in life, you would have no options or choices. And without choices or options, there would be no room for preference. There would be no room for freedom. And we each have complete freedom in every moment to choose happiness or dysphoria, no matter what the circumstances.

When people talk about freedom, they are usually thinking about freedom of action. Freedom of action is your ability to choose one set of circumstances or behaviors over another. Freedom of action is about creating your environment and the world around you. This is an important kind of freedom, but it's not quite as important as the other kind of freedom — freedom of thought and focus. This second kind of freedom is bigger and better than the first kind of freedom because it's always accessible and always guaranteed to everyone all the time, no matter what condition or circumstance they find themselves in. You always have the freedom to choose what you focus on and what you think. And because your thoughts and your focus color your feelings, you are always free to choose freedom or bondage, happiness or unhappiness, euphoria or dysphoria. You have complete control over your mood all day, every day.

A Caveat about Positive Expectations

If you want to be happy, continue to hold those positive intentions and expectations for your future and the future of your friends and family members. But remember what you learned about the principle of nonattachment in chapter 4. Don't attach your happiness to particular outcomes or specific results. Realize that things can work out in thousands of great ways. Your job is to stay open-minded, flexible, and appreciative enough to recognize the knock of opportunity or good fortune when it comes. Not all gifts come in pretty packages.

⌣∴∾

INSIDE-OUT HAPPINESS HABITS

✓ *See the value of adversity*. Notice the strengths adversity reveals. Recognize and appreciate the relationships that are left behind and the ones that remain and are strengthened. Let the adversity help you uncover what's most important in your life.

✓ *Remember that every trial or tribulation is just another opportunity for you to decide who you really want to be.* When you're experiencing adversity, ask yourself this question: "Who do I want to be in response to this problem or situation?"

✓ *Notice and appreciate the life energy that comes from unsatisfied desire.* Appreciate it for what it inspires within you. Feel the aliveness of it.

✓ *Choose happy over realistic.* Don't let adversity undermine your optimism about the future, even if having low expectations seems logical. Do this in every discussion you have, either with yourself or with others. Choose happiness in every moment you can.

9

Acting from Inspiration

A secret's value lies not in what you know, but in what you do because of what you know. Knowing the secrets or keys of happiness is useless if you don't apply them. The greatest challenge in life is to turn being into doing. Happy people don't just think and speak in ways that are happiness producing; they do things that make them happy, too. As Oliver Cromwell once said, "Not only strike while the iron is hot, but make it hot by striking."

Find a Positive Feeling First

Above all else, happy people — and successful people, too — reach for a positive feeling before they act (as long as circumstances and timing permit). Happy people always take the emotional journey first and the action journey second. Any other approach is backward and counterproductive. When you pave the way with the appropriate emotional journey, the action comes from an inspired place of happiness and centeredness, is more creative and productive, and will lead to better, more successful life outcomes.

Practice good-feeling thoughts and then follow that up with good-feeling action, behavior that is in complete alignment with those good-feeling thoughts. For instance, if you want to attract a healthier, fitter body, you won't eat "bad food" if you believe that it is not in alignment with what you want. And you can tell that a particular food isn't in alignment with your thoughts and larger intention by noticing how you feel when you consider the action of eating it. Notice how you feel and then do everything you can to turn those thoughts around. Then follow those good-feeling thoughts up with the appropriate behavior. Eventually, one day, the thought of eating that burger will not bring you the kind of resistant, guilt-ridden anxiety that it did before and it will not lead to the action that causes the weight gain and health consequences either.

Setting Goals

Goals of some kind are the basis for most of our action in the world. Inspired action, therefore, requires that you give some thought to your most fundamental goals, the ones that are the deepest touchstones of much of your behavior. Once you identify these goals and prioritize them in accordance with inside-out happiness, goal setting becomes part of the process of reaching for a positive feeling before you act.

Based on what you've read so far, you might assume that I'm not a big proponent of goals. That's only partly true. Specifically, I'm not a big fan of *extrinsic* goals. Extrinsic goals are goals that are realized in the external world, outside the psyche. Common extrinsic goals include wealth, social recognition, praise, and fame. Usually, extrinsic goals don't bring you a lot of joy in and of themselves. In most cases, the happiness derived from extrinsic goals comes only when the journey is completed successfully; it does not, by and large, come from any joy experienced on the journey itself.

While I'm not a big proponent of extrinsic goals, I am a big fan of *intrinsic* goals. Intrinsic goals involve satisfying inherent psychological needs, such as the need to belong and the need to be helpful to others. The satisfaction of intrinsic goals tends to be both pleasurable and meaningful. Remember, happiness comes from experiencing both pleasure and meaning. You combine both elements to create a full life. Happiness is not an either-or proposition. You don't have to choose between pleasure and meaning. Choose both, day after day, moment to moment.

Intrinsic goals are goals that are pursued as ends in and of themselves and not as means to some kind of external validation. Intrinsic goals are more likely to bring greater levels of happiness because they are more inspiring and enjoyable. And because they are intrinsically satisfying, they are also more likely to be accomplished because they are more easily, effortlessly, and enjoyably pursued. You will tend to persist in pursuing them. Some extrinsic goals do help in the achievement of intrinsic goals; these kinds of extrinsic goals can bring happiness, too.

Pursuing intrinsic goals means pursuing authentic goals. These are goals that speak to who you really are and what you really want, not what others want or what society says you should want. You will be happier, healthier, and harder working when you follow authentic goals.

I also strongly encourage you to make your goals approach goals, not avoidance goals. Any particular goal can be conceived of as an approach goal or an avoidance goal. An avoidance goal is aimed at escaping or removing something bad in your life. It's based in fear. An approach goal is different. It is aimed at creating or improving something in your life. It's based in love and appreciation. People who pursue avoidance goals are less happy, more anxious, and less healthy than those who pursue approach goals. That's because in pursuing an avoidance goal you have to consider so many paths at once. Almost anything could be a manifestation of what you want to avoid, whereas an approach goal has a single identifiable route. Focusing on avoidance goals may also lead you to think pessimistically, play into the negativity bias, and make you hypersensitive to threats and danger. And your pessimism could become self-fulfilling.

The overall point of this discussion is to encourage you to have goals for goals' sake, more than for any other reason.

Happy people strive for striving's sake. Pursuing dreams is critical to happiness and therefore to success. But goals are important not so much for accumulating things, accomplishing things, or getting things done as for bringing meaning, structure, and pleasure to our lives. That is, goals provide purpose and a sense of control over our lives. Pursuing goals also bolsters our self-esteem. Plus, the accomplishment of each subgoal gives us an emotional boost. Finally, pursuing goals involves engaging with other people, and social bonds are happiness inducing. When you are connected, you are closer and more aware of opportunities. In establishing goals, then, work toward intrinsic goals instead of extrinsic ones because intrinsic goals bring greater happiness and greater accomplishment and success, too.

Taking Action

Sometimes when I talk about entertaining empowered thoughts and using appreciative language, people think that I'm telling them not to take action. Nothing could be further from the truth. I am not encouraging you to rub two sticks together to create fire, to cure cancer without chemotherapy or surgery or research, to achieve world peace by sitting at home in your basement contemplating it, or to feed the world's hungry without the help of technological innovation. I am not encouraging you to lock yourself up and imprison your body just so that you can build psychological resilience or learn to be a more positive thinker.

I am not encouraging you against action in the least.

This book didn't write itself and your life won't live itself. You were not born into a physical body to live a strictly and exclusively nonphysical existence. You must take action, too. If that action is seeing a medical professional when you're sick, an athletic trainer when you're out of shape, or a financial professional when your credit is bad, that's what it means. Happiness is created by squeezing the juice out of the entire lemon, not just the core. Happy people nurture their entire beings; they nurture their bodies and souls, in addition to their minds. We must learn to take care of our bodies, possessions, finances, professional lives, personal lives, spiritual lives, and relationships, too.

But, take the emotional journey first. Then take the action journey when it is inspired and unfolds naturally from a place of inspiration and joy. If you try to reverse this process — taking an outside-in approach (do-have-feel) instead of an inside-out approach (feel-have-do) — you will never be able to take enough action to compensate for misaligned or misguided thought and emotion. The consequences will show the evidence of this law every single time.

By exploiting this single theme alone — by deliberately reaching for better-feeling thoughts and actively taking better-feeling action — you can turn your life around. Please remember, however, that these recommendations are just that — recommendations. At the end of the day, there is no one way to happiness. Happiness is the way. If you put yourself and happiness first, you'll make up the rules as you go, you'll move like sound and echo, without any deliberation. Stay liquid, stay loose, and be formless. Use what works and lose what doesn't. Most of all just keep leaning in the direction of what feels good. The rest will largely take care of itself.

~:~

INSIDE-OUT HAPPINESS HABITS

✓ *Reach for better-feeling thoughts before you act.*
✓ *Pursue intrinsic goals, goals that are rewarding in and of themselves.* Have goals for goals' sake, not for what they will net you.
✓ *Set approach goals, not avoidance goals.* Seek goals that inspire you with love and inspiration, not ones that motivate you with fear, punishment, and retribution.

Empowering Yourself and Others through Relationship

Once you get rid of the idea that you must please other people before you please yourself, and you begin to follow your own instincts — only then can you be successful. You become more satisfied, and when you are, other people tend to be satisfied by what you do.

— RAQUEL WELCH

Remember the movie *Jerry Maguire?* Tom Cruise plays Jerry Maguire, a typical sports agent who is willing to do just about anything to get the biggest possible contracts for his clients, plus a nice commission for himself. Then, one day, he suddenly has second thoughts about what he's really doing. When he voices these doubts, he ends up losing his job and all of his clients, except for Rod Tidwell, an egomaniacal football player. He also manages to retain his administrative assistant, Dorothy (played by Renée Zellweger), with whom he has a passionate, if tumultuous, relationship.

If you remember the movie, you probably remember the often quoted line and most memorable scene, in which Jerry, in a last-ditch effort to save their relationship, tracks down Dorothy, who is in the process of moving out of their shared house. After a heated exchange, Jerry says to her, "I love you. You ... you complete me."

That one notion — that somebody else can or will complete you — is probably responsible for more pain and suffering in the world than any other. If you don't feel whole and secure and happy with who you are, nobody else can ever make you whole, secure, or happy. It just doesn't work that way.

As you know if you've done any flying, the airlines are required to review the safety information for you before the airplane can take off. Part of this is the instruction "Please secure your own oxygen mask before securing the masks of those around you." The first time I heard that as a kid at the age of about eleven, it just about blew me away. How could they say that? That's so selfish! Are they basically saying that, in case of a major life-threatening crash in the Atlantic, it's every man, woman, and child for him- or herself? I was crushed. And I had more questions about where the mask was and how to get to it than any other kid on the planet. I didn't want to be sucked out of the airplane without any oxygen.

Now, of course, I've flown so many times and heard them say it so many times that the oxygen mask instruction doesn't get my attention anymore. What's so interesting about this safety instruction, however, is that it speaks directly to the concept of self-empowerment, which is the heart of my philosophy on relationships. And the way I reacted to the instruction as a kid is probably the same way you are going to react to my relationship-building recommendation: with distaste and then fear. But stay tuned in, because I eventually figured it out and you will, too.

All Relationships Are in Your Head

Relationships matter. One of the most important factors determining your happiness is the quality of your relationships — the relationships you have with others and the relationship you have with yourself. But of the two, the relationship you have with yourself is the more important. As Maxwell Maltz said, "If you make friends with yourself you will never be alone." That comment speaks volumes. When you make friends with yourself, you begin a love affair that lasts a lifetime.

Remember what I said earlier in the book about what I did when I began to turn my life around. When I moved to Miami, I made friends with myself. I took myself to the movies, expensive dinners, spas, the club, bowling, and anywhere and everywhere I wanted others to take me or accompany me. I treated myself the way I wanted to be treated by others. I talked to myself the way I wanted others to talk to me (not out loud, of course). I pampered myself the way I wanted others to pamper me. I loved myself the way I wanted others to love me. Interestingly enough, people were begging to come with me before long. People were mirroring back to me the love and appreciation I had for myself. It was so organic and, might I add, unexpected. Self-love is the prerequisite for loving others.

Most people look for love, like happiness, in all the wrong places. There is an old joke about a drunk who is frantically searching under a streetlight for something. When a passerby stops to ask the man what he is doing, the man responds that he is looking for his keys. When the passerby asks the man where he dropped the keys, the man points down the street. Not understanding, the passerby asks the man why he isn't looking for his keys down the street where they were lost. In response, the drunken man explains that it's too dark to see them down there where he dropped them, so he's decided to look for them under the streetlight, where it is brighter and he can see.

Looking for people to love you is like looking for a set of keys under a streetlight instead of where you dropped them. In the same way that many people search for happiness through financial, professional, spiritual, or physical success of some sort, many people search for love through other people. The problem is that other people never really hold the key to your heart or your happiness. No kind of success, romantic success included, will ever rescue you from your unhappy plight. Happiness and unhappiness are not out in the world; they are in you. Likewise, the love and appreciation that you seek does not exist out there in the world; it's hiding inside you. When you learn to mine the love, appreciation, sensuality, and happiness that have been sitting inside you all along, you won't go searching for ways to get them from somebody else. Then, when the right relationship does come along, you'll come to it from a much more self-sufficient, independent, and happy place.

Relationships, as you may have noticed, magnify whatever is there already. If there is unhappiness there, you feel greater unhappiness much of the time; if there is happiness there, you feel greater happiness. When you get happy first and make nothing more important than feeling good, the right relationship for you will develop. The scientific evidence backs this up. Plus, when the right relationship does develop, you will find yourself more easily turning your stumbling blocks — the insecurities, power dynamics, games, and other issues that plague most relationships — into stepping-stones, opportunities to express greater love, appreciation, and freedom. As a result, your happiness will only be added to. It, and that of your partner, will grow exponentially.

The 36th Chamber of Happiness

One of my favorite movies is called *The 36th Chamber of Shaolin*. It's a kung fu movie. I don't watch a lot of kung fu movies, but I like this one because the premise is just so relevant to what I do and what I believe. The movie follows a young man who seeks training in kung fu from one of the best schools of kung fu in the world, the Shaolin temple. Initially, the Buddhist monks reject him because he is an outsider. Eventually, however, the chief abbot sympathizes with him and lets him stay to pursue his martial arts training. As he finds out, there are thirty-five tests that he needs to pass in order to fully complete his training, and each test takes place in a particular chamber. He also learns that it is only in the thirty-fifth chamber that any real fighting is done.

As the movie proceeds, we see the young man progress through each chamber of the temple. The tasks become increasingly more difficult and require increasingly more developed and refined skill. The young student — surprising all the other students but not any of the masters — advances more rapidly than any student before him. He's so good, in fact, that he learns to create his own unique fighting tool — a three-section staff — which allows him to become a better fighter than ever before.

Once he finishes his training and completes all thirty-five chambers, he serves a short stint outside the temple where he spends time teaching common people martial arts. Soon thereafter, he returns to the Shaolin temple and establishes the most difficult but elite chamber of all, the thirty-sixth chamber. The thirty-sixth chamber is a special martial arts class designed for common people who want to learn kung fu without having to become a monk first.

I like the idea of the thirty-six chambers because the way they build on each other is similar to the way the eight principles of happiness outlined in this book build on each other and become progressively more challenging and important. The principle of self-empowerment in relationships is like the thirty-sixth chamber in the Shaolin temple because it is the most difficult to master and the greatest test of your ability to practice inside-out happiness. And if relationships are the thirty-sixth chamber of happiness, then self-sufficiency is your three-section staff.

Seeking love and appreciation through other people is no different from trying to find happiness through other people and other things. Success in any form — financial, professional, spiritual, and especially romantic — won't lead to lasting happiness, and it won't lead to lasting love, either. If chasing the various kinds of success or pleasure is a dyslexic search for happiness, then chasing romantic success is a dyslexic search for love and appreciation.

There is only one kind of love, and that is unconditional love. Hoping or wanting somebody to be different or better in any way so that you can be happy or happier puts you in a helpless state of mind and a powerless state of being. Learn to love others unconditionally. Don't ask them to be different. Look for and find the best in them and leave the other stuff out of the picture or equation. Live and let live.

Remember the law of expectation and the law of choices. Detach from the need or expectation for people to think, speak, or act in a certain way in order for you to be happy. Don't build your happiness on how you expect others to behave. Accept and love everybody for who and what they are, without asking them to be different. That doesn't mean that you'll necessarily condone or approve of their every behavior. It just means that you build your happiness on your behavior, not theirs.

If you feel negative emotion, such as disappointment, anger, frustration, or resentment, you can be sure that you've been basing your happiness on some promise or expectation that you've created, that you've made up in your own head. Even if the other person has promised or guaranteed you something, remember that the law of choices still holds true: every person has the right to choose what he or she thinks, says, and does. He or she can, at any point in time, break that promise or expectation. As long as you haven't built your happiness on the fulfillment of the expectation or promise, your happiness will not be in jeopardy.

How many times have you gotten mad or frustrated when somebody wouldn't call or write you back right away or at all? How often have you been upset and angry that somebody wouldn't change his behavior to suit your needs by, for example, picking up after himself, complaining less, coming to visit you more often, changing his political views, changing his diet, or appreciating you more?

What you forget is that (1) you don't get to make the decision to change the other person's behavior, because that's his decision, and (2) your happiness depends on your thoughts, words, and actions, and those are decisions or choices you always have complete control over. Once you approach your relationships with these simple truths in mind, your happiness will begin soaring. Detach from the need for anybody to be different or better in order for you to be better. Live and let live. In relationships as in life, detachment is the key to authentic, lasting unconditional happiness.

You Teach People How to Treat You

The relationship you have with yourself sets the tone for all other relationships in your life. You teach people how to treat you. When you understand that you set the precedent for your relationships by the way you treat yourself, you learn to start treating yourself and talking to yourself in more supportive ways. And you realize that it's never up to anybody else to make you feel better about you. Remember, all experiences are filtered through your own perception and shaped by your own beliefs. So, ultimately, you always determine how any particular relationship affects you and makes you feel. It's all in your head. Every relationship you have is in your mind.

Eleanor Roosevelt was only half right. It's true that no one can make you feel inferior without your consent; but it's also true that no one can make you feel anything at all without your consent. The only person who can hurt or disappoint or betray or frustrate you is you. Likewise, the only person who can fulfill, satisfy, impress, delight, inspire, or empower you is you. You are the vortex through which emotion flows.

When you really think about it, all problems are caused by not loving yourself. Loving yourself is the most important thing you can do, because when you love yourself, hurting others isn't necessary to feel better about yourself. And what other people think of you is not your business and it's not your work. Through their thoughts, they create their experiences. And through your thoughts, you create your experiences.

When you have made what you feel on the inside more important than the opinions, voices, and peanut gallery of advice on the outside, you have mastered your life. You cannot get into the mind of a single other person, much less those of six billion others. You cannot stand on your head in enough different ways to make everybody happy.

You must learn to make how you feel the most important thing in the world, your dominant intent every day. Take everybody else and how they feel out of the equation. What others do has nothing to do with you. Although they may be well meaning, others may attempt to coerce or coax you away from your own emotional compass and well-being because they are following their own unique emotional compasses. Learn to tease out your own goals from the goals of your friends, family, and society. Pursue your own goals and leave everybody else's goals to them. Consider the social norms that are influencing what you want. Think about what you really want.

Does this make you fearful that others will call you selfish because they'd selfishly prefer that you accommodate their needs? Well, the truth of the matter is that authentically, consciously, deliberately happy people are not selfish. They are the most altruistic, unconditionally loving, compassionate, generous people in the world.

Selflessly Happy

Once you've chosen happiness as your goal, you don't need to worry about being selfish. Indeed, the either-or situation suggested by the concepts of "selfish" and "selfless" becomes a false dichotomy. Studies show that congenitally happy people are nicer and tend to volunteer more often. They are friendlier, more generous, and more helpful. Happiness leads to greater compassion.

The relationship between kindness and happiness is reciprocal. Happiness makes people kinder, and kindness makes people happier, too. Research has found that giving blood makes people feel good about themselves and that the more people volunteer, the higher they score on measures of happiness and well-being. The effect seems to be mediated by bringing people together and by facilitating and providing content for the creation of a meaningful life story.

In their book *Why Good Things Happen to Good People*, Stephen Post and Jill Neimark report that giving protects overall health twice as much as aspirin protects against heart disease. They explain that giving in high school predicts good physical health and mental health fifty years later, reduces mortality, and reduces adolescent depression and suicide risk. Giving also helps us to forgive ourselves for our own mistakes and may help us gain a sense of control over our lives. So, one of my inside-out happiness tips is this: if you are not feeling joy yourself, help someone else feel it.

Happy people are not selfish people. On the contrary, they are selfless. And happy people are self-aware enough to make happiness their dominant intent, their top priority. Likewise, they are conscious enough to know that authentic happiness comes from — can only come from — the inside out. You can't give what you don't have. And happy people have a lot of love and a lot of joy. They share it with others because it makes them feel good. And because it makes them feel good, they share it with others.

Think in Terms of Empowerment, Not Charity

Sometimes people think they can help others by feeling bad with or for them. Sometimes we think that ratcheting back our happiness or joy will somehow help a friend or partner in need. But you are never helping another by feeling bad, because you only exacerbate the other person's feeling of lack and, hence, influence him or her to attract more of both the feeling and the resulting consequences of that feeling. And you do the same for yourself. Compassion is one thing. Empathy, however, is quite another. While happy people are deeply compassionate and even sympathetic, very rarely do they let circumstances and conditions permanently defeat them. Know that no amount of unhappiness or empathetic understanding will ever bring you, your friends, or your family greater happiness.

You can't get unhappy enough to help a depressed spouse or friend. You can't get poor enough to feed the hungry or house the homeless. You can't get lonely enough to make a love connection for yourself or any other person. Remember that words don't teach; only experience teaches. We teach best by example.

To help others, be happy. And see them as happy. You cannot give what you do not have. Do not think that, in lowering your vibration, you are helping them. You are not. You are disempowering them, and they (and their problems) will eventually consume you. Their problems will become your own. Do not see others as broken and in need of fixing, or helpless and in need of help. See them as whole and in working order. Then think in terms of empowerment, not charity. When in doubt, leave people alone when they are in a low mood.

Secure your own oxygen mask first, and then you can much more effectively, efficiently, and frequently help those around you. You can't successfully help anyone if you're asphyxiating or dead. And you can't — and won't — effectively help anyone if you're miserable. It just doesn't work that way.

Self-Empowerment in Practice

Derrick is a professional athlete and a client of mine. Some years ago, his sister became dependent on him for money. Derrick thought that he should have some say over how she spent the money that he loaned her. He called me to help him diplomatically solve this familial conflict.

I asked Derrick to envision his sister as strong, independent, and self-sufficient before every interaction or meeting he had with her. He had some trouble doing this in the beginning but he got better with time. I told him not to try to change his behavior toward her but only to pre-pave his visits and conversations with this simple visualization exercise.

Once he built momentum in this direction, I encouraged Derrick to let his behavior and conversations with his sister follow naturally from this place of seeing his sister as powerful, independent, and self-sufficient. Interestingly enough, Derrick stopped lending his sister money all the time because he saw that she wasn't broken and didn't need fixing, and he realized that his money was disempowering her, not supporting her true long-term desires. Instead, he found other, more empowering ways to support her, such as helping to find her a new, better-paying job that used her natural talents and strengths and paying for her to hire credit counselors and attend financial seminars. He referred her to staffing companies and helped her establish a budget. Whenever Derrick felt any resistance on her behalf, he let up because he knew that she was smart and capable and would figure it out on her own eventually. Derrick's sister now runs her own small but successful credit restoration clinic and Derrick's money is making money for him, too.

Focus on Strengths

Your value does not rest in your ability to shore up weaknesses, to address deficiency, or to fix what is broken in yourself or anybody else. You do yourself and others a disservice when you believe that you live in a broken world and that others are broken. You cannot focus on the weaknesses of yourself or somebody else and expect or encourage any kind of strength or power. You cannot focus on what you or somebody else is doing wrong and think that that will engender the right action and will make you feel any better. No, instead you have to focus on what is working, what is right. You have to focus on strengths. You have to focus on what makes you feel good when you focus on it. And when you do that, your entire life and those of the people around you will turn in the direction of those thoughts, shifting from negative to positive like a tide.

In fact, by building on your unique strengths and by helping others to build on their unique strengths, you can learn and teach others how to spend a lot more time in flow, joy, and happiness. In every situation and in every individual, there are some things that are already working and some things that aren't working. Happy people find what's working and exploit it. They create flow experiences and live absorbed and engaging lives. They also perform better and are, therefore, more successful because they persevere, lose track of time, and become less self-conscious and, hence, less self-destructive. They get out of their own way.

To ensure a happy relationship with yourself and with others, then, focus on the strengths as opposed to the weaknesses of both yourself and your partner. Exploit what's already working.

Interestingly enough, science has found that positive illusions make for happier relationships. In fact, the bigger the positive discrepancy between the image that you have of your partner and the image that the partner's friends have, the more stable and happy your relationship will be. Contrariwise, the most dissatisfied people create tainted images and see fewer virtues in their partners than the partner's friends see. Further, all but one combination of pessimists and optimists allow some probability of success in a marriage: two pessimists. If you want to have the happiest relationship, then, focus on your partner's strengths and what he or she does well, not his or her weaknesses, foibles, and character flaws.

Get happy first, authentically and unconditionally happy. And stay happy. Everything else will follow from that accordingly. As you look for things to appreciate in others, you will find yourself buried in appreciative relationships.

Happily Ever After

As I noted at the beginning of this book, married people in general are happier people. However, they are not happier because they are married. While marriage itself does offer a slight, temporary bump in happiness ratings, statistically speaking, that initial bump does not last; married individuals eventually return to their original happiness baseline, the same happiness that they experienced before getting married. So, "wedded bliss" does exist but it exists only to the extent that you are happy before meeting that special someone.

So, it seems, the happiest relationships are built by happy individuals. And happy individuals, as we have learned, make happiness their dominant intent, their top priority, and their ultimate currency above all else. They detach their happiness from specific results or outcomes, find reasons to feel good and things to appreciate, tell better-feeling but believable stories about their lives and the world based in truth, embrace adversity, learn and practice optimism.

The Bottom Line

My advice about relationships is the same advice I give about living in general. Make happiness your top priority. Remember that nobody else and nothing else can ever make you feel whole or secure or happy. That is both your responsibility and your opportunity. Give up the Jerry Maguire complex. Detach from specific outcomes or results and you'll give up the expectation hangovers that result. Look for, focus on, think about, and talk about what you appreciate and the best of what exists in your life and the lives of those people around you. Move toward better-feeling people and away from worse-feeling people. Especially beware of happiness regulators and energy vampires, those people who make you feel worse about life in general, and your life or yourself in particular. And remember, above all else, to judge your relationships by how they make you feel, not how long they last. That is, judge your relationships not by their length, but by their depth.

If, in your relationships and your life in general, you reach for a positive, appreciative feeling before you speak and act, your words and actions will produce the freshest, most delicious fruit. The appropriate action will always be inspired naturally from a place of joy and well-being and your happiness will grow exponentially as a result, from the inside out.

◡∶◠

INSIDE-OUT HAPPINESS HABITS

✓ *Make your happiness your job, not your partner's.* Don't rely on relationships to make you feel complete. Give up the Jerry Maguire complex.

✓ *Mind your own business; stay on your side of the road.* Don't try to convert anybody to your point of view. And don't care so much what other people think.

✓ *To best help others and yourself, focus on strengths.* When you feel joy, you give joy to the world. Think in terms of empowerment, not charity.

✓ *Move toward better-feeling people and away from worse-feeling people.*

11

A Storybook Ending

I'm not sad it's over, I'm glad it happened.

— DR. SEUSS

Imagine a little kid at an amusement park. He's been waiting nine years to finally ride this incredible roller coaster at his favorite amusement park. Every year before, he's been too short. But he never let it get him down. Every year, all year long, he's thought about the ride. He's imagined the whole experience. And he's done everything within his power to make himself tall enough to go on the ride. He's eaten right and stretched himself out like Michael Jordan on monkey bars. This year he's finally tall enough. He gets in line. The line is very long. Strangely, he finds the line moves almost too fast for him. He's so excited at the mere prospect of riding this roller coaster and he's been bathing in the excitement so intensely that he doesn't even notice when it's his turn. The attendant has to call him three or four times. "Next! Next rider, please!" The boy has worked himself into such a tizzy he's not even quite ready to be on the ride. It's not that he is the least bit scared or nervous. He's been preparing for the ride for nine full years. He's just so excited about fulfilling his desire that he's quite happy prolonging the moments of anticipation. Finally, he gets on and takes off! When he's done, he jumps off enthusiastically. "Wow," he says, "that was almost as good as I imagined it to be!"

As you strive to be happier in your life, think about the boy at the amusement park. Grab hold of your mind's tremendous ability to imagine the roller-coaster ride ahead. Feed off the energy of the anticipation, but — and this is the crux of it all — make peace with where you are by finding things to appreciate right here and right now.

Excuse Me, Your Happiness and Success Are Waiting

The first step to creating a happier, more successful life is to make peace with where you are. It's only where you are. It's only a platform. Find things to appreciate. Make lists of them. Find reasons to feel good. Fill your life with them. Then make sure that every one of your thoughts, words, and ac-tions furthers and enhances that peace you've made with the present, that appreciative stance you've taken, and that blissful being you've awakened. When every thought, word, and action supports and empowers your vision of happiness, not only will you have created a happy life, but you will have found uncommon success as well.

Be persistent. Practice, and I promise you'll get better. Great masters choose the same thing day in and day out. There's no wavering, doubting, indecision, or confusion. There's just perseverance and confidence.

I remember going fishing with my grandfather, my father, and my brother, Brant. We rented a couple of little rowboats, I think. And I'll never forget what my father and grandfather said to my brother and me. Almost in unison, they said, "What the hell are you two boys doing over there? Why do you keep pulling your line and bait out of the water? We're not fly-fishing, boys! Leave your line in the water. If you stop moving it around so damn much, you'll stop scaring all the fish away, and then maybe you'll finally catch something instead of hooking each other! Be patient. You think you're saving yourself time by moving it around but all you're really doing is wasting energy, splitting your focus, and rocking the boat. So just throw it in there and leave it! You're working too damn hard!" You had to hear the tone in their voices to really get this. Their voices were full of love, compassion, humor, and perhaps just a touch of sarcasm. I'll never forget that. I'll always love them for what they said and how they said it.

Learn to be more present. Making peace with the present means finding things in your life and reality to appreciate now. Be here now. Be easy about life. Don't rush into things, out of things, or through things. Life isn't a sprint. Savor things more. Most of all, put all your energy, attention, and intention into finding that which brings you meaning and pleasure. Let your desire to feel good be your lighthouse, your shining star, your compass. If you always recruit and practice thoughts, words, and actions that feel good, you will always experience happiness and you will always attract good-feeling things. Good will come to you, just as good comes from you.

Everything you will ever want or need is available to you. All you have to do is practice thinking appreciative thoughts, words, and actions. There is nothing you cannot be or do or have.

Through all of it, keep the faith. Know and trust that the better you feel, the greater the chances that better-feeling things are on their way to you. Science says so. Enhance and exaggerate those positive feelings by looking for evidence and proof that things are working out. As part of that, it sometimes helps to remember that good things are usually long on their way to you before you see any proof of it. The job is yours long before you actually receive the offer letter or get the phone call. Your new mate is on his or her way to you long before you meet him or her. The money you want is on its way to you long before you actually see it show up in your mailbox. If you believe it, you will see it. If you need to see proof or evidence before you believe it, you'll have to wait for somebody else to create the evidence before you can believe it. And there's no power or freedom in depending on others to make you happy. As Martin Luther King Jr. once said, "Take the first step in faith. You don't have to see the whole staircase. Just take the first step."

A Happy Ending to a Happy Journey

It's been a brilliant journey of self-awakening. And now you've simply got to ask yourself this: What is happiness to me?

As we wrap up our time here together, I would like to leave you with a thought on happiness. When you were a kid, you were sure that each shiny new bicycle, new basketball, or pretty new doll was all you would need to be happy. Before you knew it, you had three of each sitting around, rusting, deflating, or decaying before your eyes. As you grew older, you moved on to new dreams and fresh fantasies, adult-sized ones like going out with that hot new boy or girl, getting into that prestigious university, or owning that shiny new car. "If I could only get that," you believed, "I'd be happy forever and ever." Not too much later, you were left heartbroken, the car's paint was beginning to fade, and you realized that college required a lot more hard work than you planned for.

At some point in your life, you may have convinced yourself that life would be better after you got married, had a baby, or had another baby. Then you were frustrated that the kids weren't old enough to do for themselves and seek their own happiness. After that, you may have been frustrated that you had teenagers to deal with. You will certainly be happy, you told yourself, when they are out of that stage. You may have told yourself that your life will be complete when your spouse gets his or her act together, when you get a nicer car, when you are able to go on a nice vacation, or when you retire.

The truth is there's no better time to be happy than right now. There never has been, and never will be, a happy ending to an unhappy journey. If not now, when? Your life will always be filled with challenges. It's best to admit this to yourself and decide to be happy anyway. Happiness is the way. So, treasure every moment that you have and treasure it more because you made a decision to do so. Remember that time waits for no one.

Stop waiting. Happiness is here now, waiting inside you, waiting to be seized and used.

Acknowledgments

First of all, I'd like to thank my mother (Donna Guinn) and father (Robert G. Mack) who have loved and provided for me in ways that no other human beings ever could. Thank you for your unconditional love, support, and infinite guidance. Your generosity, compassion, and kindness have no bounds; your wisdom knows no limits. Thank you for leading me back to myself and my own internal guidance system.

Brant Mack: thank you for being my best friend and closest, most loyal fan. I love you deeply and I believe in you more than you will ever believe in yourself. You won't be successful. You already are.

Angela Mack: thank you for being my best advocate. Thank you for always being a source of boundless energy, limitless enthusiasm, and bottomless inspiration. You are a testament to what happens when someone finds something to be enthusiastic about, drives her life with commitment, dedication, integrity, and passion, and channels God-force to undauntingly steer through adversity.

161

Vanessa Williams and family: thank you for being such a driving force in my life, both personally and professionally. Your confidence, love, and bottomless patience leave me inspired, awestruck, and deeply, deeply moved. I've become a better person each additional day that I've known you. Thank you, too, for sharing, and continuing to share, your family, your friends, your love, and your life with me. Your love and kindness are indelibly etched on my heart.

Chris Williams: thank you for your confidence and your understanding. Most of all, thank you for encouraging me to write this book.

Dorothy Granger, Denise Granger, Tod Granger, and family: thank you, Denise, for your understanding and patience; thank you, Tod, for your ageless wisdom, intelligent guidance, and unconditional support; and thank you, Dorothy, for your unmatched flexibility, endless understanding, unparalleled patience, and unconditional love and regard. My life is forever changed for the better for knowing all of you; my soul is inscribed with the impression you have made.

Adam Belanoff: thank you for your confidence and your public expressions of support. I'm better for knowing you. Thank you, also, for sharing your talents with all of us.

Lisa McCourt: thank you for being the voice of reason and clarity amidst a whirling wind of confusion and madness. Thank you for believing in me so resolutely, for sharing yourself so unabashedly, and for getting to know me and my writing so intimately.

Jerry and Esther Hicks, Wayne Dyer, Byron Katie, Lisa Nichols, Eckhart Tolle, Marianne Williamson, and Louise Hay: thank you all for being my best virtual friends and most loving and honest critics from a distance in the times of my deepest desperation, most intense solitude, and most serious sadness.

Thanks for inspiring me to turn my biggest trials and tribulations into my greatest triumphs by following my heart and not my head.

Bruce Rogol and family: thank you for introducing me to myself all over again. Thank you for practicing what you preach. Thank you for your timeless wisdom, loyal support, and unconditional love. Just thinking about you, who you are, what you've done, and where you're going makes me feel sublimely heady and blissfully happy. Thank you for not asking me to apologize for who I am or what I do.

Andrew Ward, Barry Schwartz, James Pawelski, Marty Seligman, Judy Salzberg, and Karen Reivich: thank you for helping me to ground common sense and intuitive understanding in tried-and-true scientific evidence. Thank you, too, for helping me to bring passion, emotion, and the romantic to reason, science, and the somewhat sterile. Thank you also for forgiving any empirical inaccuracies, scientific slip-ups, and misleading material that may be presented in this text. Thank you for understanding that I've done my best to maintain the integrity of the discipline while simultaneously trying to reach as many people as possible.

Melanie Whittle and A. J. Samonte: thank you for living out the principles in my book in your everyday lives. Thank you for providing me with a sounding board — and a soapbox — for sharing my ideas, experiences, and love.

My clients: thank you for giving me the opportunity to share what I love and believe in. Thank you for keeping an open mind and an open heart.

Georgia Hughes, Kristen Cashman, Jonathan Wichmann, and Eric Engles: thank you for doing all the heavy lifting getting this book in shape. I adore you, cherish you, and thank you over and over again for believing in this piece and for always making this book — and me and my vision — a top priority in your lives. I will not forget what you've sacrificed in this regard. I hope you feel better off for knowing me and working with me. I certainly feel that way about you.

Kim Corbin: thank you for leading this entire effort and being this book's biggest cheerleader. You've made this book a success already, and it hasn't sold a single copy yet.

Kino McGregor and Tim: thank you for providing me a safe place to fall, in the form of the Miami Life Center, your homes, and your hearts. I'm deeply appreciative of the faith that you've had and continue to have in me. My admiration of what you do daily is surpassed only by my love for you both. I look forward to personal and professional relationships that continue to grow in leaps and bounds.

Mike Dale and Ramani Durvasula: thank you for offering your balanced meliorism in the form of traditional psychological understanding. Thank you for challenging many of my tightly held, unconscious assumptions. Thank you for helping me to step out confidently in the direction of my biggest dreams.

Professor Mike Mullan: thank you for encouraging me to write — not just this book but anything at all. Thank you even more for so persuasively convincing me of my own unique gifts. I love you for that.

My readers and fans: thank you for accepting this book as my best effort thus far and understanding that a happier, healthier, and wealthier life lies not ahead of you, but inside you. Thank you, too, for hearing, above all else, that you have a good life now and that your growing awareness of that good life will bring you a better one.

Notes

Each note corresponds to the page number listed in the left-hand column.

Introduction

1   Easterbrook, Gregg, *The Progress Paradox: How Life Gets Better While People Feel Worse* (New York: Random House, 2003).

3   *"Man, I see in fight club the strongest and smartest men"*: *Fight Club*, DVD, directed by David Fincher (1999; Burbank, CA: 20th Century Fox, 2002).

9   *"like sound and echo, without any deliberation"*: Bruce Lee, *The Tao of Gung Fu: A Study in the Way of Chinese Martial Art*, ed. John Little (Boston: C. E. Tuttle, 1997), 138.

Chapter 1. My Life Is My Message

16   *"Jerry, I told you that psychiatrists don't work for me"*: *Anything Else*, DVD, directed by Woody Allen (2003; Universal City, CA: DreamWorks Home Entertainment, 2003).

Chapter 2. Authentic Happiness

28   *In fact, parents' happiness hits a low point when*: Stefan Klein, *The Science of Happiness: How Our Brains Make Us Happy — and What We Can Do to Get Happier* (New York: Marlowe, 2006), 147.

28   *There's a great Michael Bay–directed movie*: The Island, DVD, directed by Michael Bay (2005; Universal City, CA: DreamWorks Home Entertainment, 2005).

38   *"We act as though comfort and luxury"*: Charles Kingsley, quoted in John Cook, Steve Deger, and Leslie Ann Gibson, eds., *The Book of Positive Quotations* (Minneapolis: Fairview Press, 2007), 36.

39   *Not only does happiness protect against pain*: Barbara Fredrickson and Christine Branigan, "Positive Emotions Broaden the Scope of Attention and Thought-Action Repertoires," *Cognition and Emotion* 19 (2005): 313–32.

41   *"I had so much promise"*: "The Opposite," *Seinfeld: Season 5*, DVD, disc 4 (Culver City, CA: Sony Pictures Home Entertainment, 2005).

42   *Here's a list from Barry Schwartz's book*: Barry Schwartz, *The Paradox of Choice: Why More Is Less* (New York: Harper-Collins, 2005), 110.

Chapter 3. Finding Pleasure and Meaning

54   *My friend and former professor Barry Schwartz*: Barry Schwartz, *The Paradox of Choice: Why More Is Less* (New York: Harper-Collins, 2005), 110.

59   *He calls it "the Hamburger Model"*: Tal Ben-Shahar, *Happier: Learn the Secrets to Daily Joy and Lasting Fulfillment* (New York: McGraw-Hill, 2007), 14.

Chapter 4. Practicing Nonattachment

65   *Emotions are important because*: Jon Elster, *Alchemies of the Mind: Rationality and the Emotions* (Cambridge, UK: Cambridge University Press, 1999), 403.

66   *"In basketball — as in life — true joy comes from being fully present"*: Phil Jackson, quoted in Joel Weiss, ed., *The Quotable Manager: Inspiration for Business and Life* (Salt Lake City: Gibbs Smith, 2006), 236.

Chapter 5. Focusing on the Positive

79   *"Each of us makes his own weather"*: Fulton J. Sheen, quoted in John Cook, Steve Deger, and Leslie Ann Gibson, eds., *The Book of Positive Quotations* (Minneapolis: Fairview Press, 2007), 256.

81   *In one study, for instance, subjects were asked*: Daniel M. Wegner, *White Bears and Other Unwanted Thoughts: Suppression, Obsession, and the Psychology of Mental Control* (New York: Guilford Press, 1994), 207.

84   *A landmark study conducted by Walter Mischel*: Gerald Matthews, Moshe Zeidner, and Richard D. Roberts, *Emotional Intelligence: Science and Myth* (Cambridge, MA: MIT Press, 2002), 437.

Chapter 6. Appreciating Yourself

88   *A study, for instance, found Olympic bronze medalists to be happier*: Barry Schwartz, *The Paradox of Choice: Why More Is Less* (New York: HarperCollins, 2005), 150.

89   *Science has found that the benefits of being grateful*: Deborah Norville, *Thank You Power: Making the Science of Gratitude Work for You* (Nashville, TN: Thomas Nelson, 2007), 79.

92   *The result is that they are less happy*: Barry Schwartz, *The Paradox of Choice: Why More Is Less* (New York: HarperCollins, 2005), 201.

92   *The psychologist Douglas Kenrick showed women*: Douglas T. Kenrick, Steven L. Neuberg, Kristin L. Zierk, and Jacquelyn M. Krones, "Evolution and Social Cognition: Contrast Effects as a Function of Sex, Dominance, and Physical Attractiveness," *Personality and Social Psychology Bulletin* 20, no. 2 (1994): 210–17.

Chapter 7. Telling a Happier Story

101 *"Did you guys hear about that train explosion"*: "Debbie
Downer," *Saturday Night Live*, season 29, episode 18, May 1,
2004, available for viewing at http://media.putfile.com/
SNL-Debbie-Downer-WDW (accessed January 14, 2009).

102 *"I'm in a wonderful position"*: Pierre S. DuPont IV, quoted in
John Cook, Steve Deger, and Leslie Ann Gibson, eds., *The
Book of Positive Quotations* (Minneapolis: Fairview Press,
2007), 361.

103 *"The truth of a thing is the feel of it"*: Stanley Kubrick,
quoted in Cook, Deger, and Gibson, *The Book of Positive
Quotations*, 419.

112 *"Act as if you were already happy"*: Dale Carnegie, quoted
in Cook, Deger, and Gibson, *The Book of Positive
Quotations*, 360.

Chapter 8. Embracing Adversity

124 *"I have missed more than nine thousand shots"*: Michael Jordan,
quoted in Ruth Fishel, *Change Almost Anything in 21 Days:
Recharge Your Life with the Power of Over 500 Affirmations*
(Deerfield Beach, FL: Health Communications, 2003), 150.

125 *"No pessimist ever discovered the secret"*: Helen Keller, quoted in
David Ross, ed., *1,001 Pearls of Wisdom* (San Francisco:
Chronicle Books, 2006), quotation 752.

Chapter 9. Acting from Inspiration

131 *"Not only strike while the iron is hot"*: Oliver Cromwell, quoted
in Bob Kelly, ed., *Worth Repeating: More Than 5,000 Classic and
Contemporary Quotes* (Grand Rapids, MI: Kregel, 2003), 9.

136 *"Be formless...shapeless, like water"*: Bruce Lee, *The Tao of
Gung Fu: A Study in the Way of Chinese Martial Art*, ed. John
Little (Boston: C. E. Tuttle, 1997), 138.

Chapter 10. Empowering Yourself and Others through Relationship

140 *"I love you. You . . . you complete me"*: *Jerry Maguire*, DVD, directed by Cameron Crowe (1996; Culver City, CA: Sony Pictures Home Entertainment, 1997).

141 *"If you make friends with yourself you will never be alone"*: Maxwell Maltz, quoted in John Cook, Steve Deger, and Leslie Ann Gibson, eds., *The Book of Positive Quotations* (Minneapolis: Fairview Press, 2007), 233.

149 *Research has found that giving blood makes people feel good*: Stephen Post and Jill Neimark, *Why Good Things Happen to Good People: The Exciting New Research That Proves the Link between Doing Good and Living a Longer, Healthier, Happier Life* (New York: Broadway, 2007), 65–68.

149 *giving protects overall health twice as much as aspirin*: Ibid.

Chapter 11. A Storybook Ending

160 *"Take the first step in faith"*: Martin Luther King Jr., quoted in Jack Canfield and Janet Switzer, *The Success Principles: How to Get from Where You Are to Where You Want to Be* (New York: Harper Resource Books, 2005), 110.

Index

About the Author

Robert Mack entered the public eye through a career in entertainment with Wilhelmina Models. Since then he has made guest appearances on television shows for MTV, NBC, CBS, and UPN and shot commercials and advertisements for numerous clients across the world. Prior to his career in entertainment, Rob attended Swarthmore College on an academic scholarship. After graduating, Rob worked as a consultant for one of the largest consulting companies in the world, Deloitte & Touche, where he worked with international Fortune 500 companies and CEOs to help them optimize performance and satisfaction. Subsequently, Rob graduated from the University of Pennsylvania's Master of Applied Positive Psychology (MAPP) program. In addition to coaching private clients, Rob is the resident life coach for Miami Life Center, one of *Travel & Leisure* magazine's top twenty-five health and wellness centers/retreats. Rob resides in Miami, Florida.